Tales Out of School

Tales Out of School

CONTEMPORARY WRITERS ON THEIR STUDENT YEARS

EDITED BY

SUSAN RICHARDS SHREVE AND **PORTER SHREVE**

BEACON PRESS

BOSTON

BEACON PRESS
25 Beacon Street
Boston, Massachusetts 02108–2892
www.beacon.org

BEACON PRESS BOOKS
are published under the auspices of
the Unitarian Universalist Association of Congregations.

05 04 03 02 01 00   8 7 6 5 4 3 2 1

Text design by Elizabeth Elsas
Composition by Wilsted & Taylor Publishing Services

Library of Congress Cataloging-in-Publication Data
Tales out of school : contemporary writers on their student years / edited by Susan
    Richards Shreve and Porter Shreve.
        p.   cm.
    ISBN 0-8070-4216-1 (cl : acid-free paper)
        1. Authors, American—20th century—Biography.   2. Students—United
States—Biography.   3. Education—United States.   I. Shreve, Susan Richards.
II. Shreve, Porter.
    PS129.T28   2000
    810.9'0054—dc21   00-020763

CONTENTS

SUSAN RICHARDS SHREVE

Introduction

I have had half a century of an uneasy alliance with school. I have been a student of course, a bad student, a very bad student, and finally a good one. I have been a teacher of kindergarten and fourth grade and sixth grade and seventh grade and high school and undergraduates in public universities and undergraduates in private universities, a founder of an alternative school in Philadelphia for difficult-to-impossible children. And for the last twenty years a professor of English in a master of fine arts program at a large public university. I am a mother of four children—one of whom at four was asked to leave the school at which his father was headmaster; the second packed up her book bag in kindergarten, walked out the front door, crossed six streets, one major, and arrived home as the telephone was ringing with the news that she had disappeared. The third, recovering from his early elementary years as a good boy, led a four-year opposition to the administration of his school which required that I leave home early in the morning before the principal began to call with his complaints. And the fourth, a daughter, an actual committed scholar, simply didn't go to school very much at all, preferring to read *Anna Karenina* at home over and over again. It is sufficient to say that during my children's combined fifty-two years in various schools before they went off to college, I spent as many hours talking to principals, teachers, other parents, and to them about their relationship to *school* as I spent at any other job.

I am the daughter of a teacher, whose father, also a teacher, took her out of school when she was six and taught her at home until she was fifteen because she was left-handed and the school was trying to change that. At the heart of all of the pieces in *Tales Out of School* is a child who was different, who didn't exactly fit the changing definitions of institutional learning perhaps inevitable in a vast pluralistic country working its way back and forth toward democracy.

TEN TALES OUT OF SCHOOL

1. The first day of first grade and I'm sitting in the front row, chewing off the collar of the dress my mother made me, a habit I had of eating the cotton collars of several outfits a year—a condition of general agitation that would be corrected today with regular doses of Ritalin. I'm watching Mrs. Comstock, soft, plump, weary, and very old, write on the blackboard.

"Who reads?" she asks.

I put up my hand. I don't read and wonder as I look around the room whether the other students with their hands up are telling the truth.

"Good," Mrs. Comstock says, satisfied that we're off to a fine start. "I'm going to write down the rules for First Grade, Section A, Mrs. Comstock's class."

1. NO lateness
2. NO impudence
3. NO speaking out in class
4. NO whispering
5. NO bathroom visits during class
6. NO morning recess unless classwork is completed
7. NO food in the classroom
8. NO temper tantrums
9. NO pushing or shoving when you line up
10. NO tears

I'm extremely pleased as I watch the list run down the black-board. Although I can't read, do not even want to learn if it means, as I'm afraid it will, giving up the hours sitting next to my mother or father in my small bed while they read to me—I do recognize the word *NO*. I even count the number of *NO*s filling up the blackboard. There are ten.

"So," Mrs. Comstock says, turning around to face us. "Who can read me the rules?"

I don't raise my hand but there I am sitting directly in front of her and without a second's hesitation, she calls my name. I don't even stop to think.

"No, no, no, no, no, no, no, no, no, no," I say without taking a breath.

2. Checking the obituaries in the *Washington Post* as I have done forever, preferring the story of a whole life, pleased to fill in the missing spaces—I find on page three of the metro section the notice that my fifth grade teacher, age ninety-three, is dead of natural causes. Dead and I didn't know it. She slipped out of the world and I wasn't even aware of the sudden absence of danger when I woke up this morning.

I am a grown-up, forty-two with four children of my own, a responsible job as a teacher. A teacher of course, a teacher of all things.

"Why would you throw your life away?" my mother, the teacher, said to me the first year I taught school. "You could be anything and you choose to be a teacher."

I cut out the obit and tape it on the refrigerator.

"My fifth grade teacher," I say when my children ask why the death of a stranger is noted on the fridge.

Friends School, Section 5-B on the first floor next to the library. I sat in the middle of the last row between Harry Slough, who smelled of old bananas, and God's perfect creation, Toni Brewer, with her loopy blond braids and straight A's.

"I never heard you mention your fifth grade teacher to us," one of my children says to me. "Are you *very* upset?"

"Not a bit," I reply. "Only that it took so long to happen."

They look at me in horror, knowing maybe for the first time, the full measure of revenge.

The story of my fifth grade teacher goes like this:

I was going to a Quaker school selective in its choice of students, no blacks, no learning disabilities, but willing to accept the occasional handicapped child that the public schools did not. I wasn't exactly handicapped but I had had polio and when I was young I wore metal braces and went around on crutches. Children like me used to be taught at home by drop-in tutors, our social lives accommodated by regular deliveries of turkeys and gumdrops and occasional coloring books from the local Kiwanas Club, which did nothing to compensate for the lonely life of home schooling.

It was late autumn before Thanksgiving and I had been in the habit of forgetting my math homework. Maybe I didn't do it and lied about it, maybe I never did my math homework—those details I have forgotten. But this morning the fifth grade teacher noted to the class that once again I had flunked my math test.

"But," she added with a show of enduring patience, folding her arms across her military chest, "we have to be nice to little Suzie Richards because she had polio."

3. In twelfth grade, with little distinction as a student but a belief, not commonly shared, that I was a promising writer, I had Mr. Forsythe as a teacher. We all did. We'd been waiting throughout high school for this extraordinary opportunity to write under his direction. The papers were long, analytic essays in response to questions about our readings in English literature. I had in mind to rescue my academic reputation in Mr. Forsythe's senior English and was stunned as paper after paper came back to me full of red pencil and paragraphs of criticism written in his tiny, crabbed hand with D+ and C− and D and D and D.

"I suppose you think I'm a terrible writer," I said when I finally went into his office.

He looked up under hooded eyes, an expression of unspeakable boredom on his face. "You make up your answers," he replied. "These questions require research."

*   *   *

4. I am twenty-two living in England and I'm hired to teach what would be fourth grade at a school in a working-class community across the river from Liverpool. These students are hard-core tough, raised on cowboy movies where they've learned a new vocabulary— *ain't,* for example. There are forty of them and I have never taught school. The only thing I'm told before I walk into the makeshift classroom, two to a desk, is that caning in England is against the law. Of course, I think. I have a Dickensian view of caning, the craggy, long-faced wet-eyed master beating the child to smithereens with a heavy cane.

My despair as a teacher focuses on Lily Diamond, a small, plump, vacant child who has it in mind to drive me crazy. Maybe sixty times a day, she falls off her chair, turns upside down, her legs in the air, screaming, "Ain't, ain't, ain't, ain't," while the rest of the class goes wild with excitement. I have absolutely no control.

It has come to my attention that in the top drawer of my desk there is a small stick, not much longer than a pencil, the same width and hollow like a reed. I have begun to imagine this stick applied to the bottom of Lily Diamond. And one Wednesday during math, right in the middle of a chorus of "ain'ts" from the floor, I take out the stick, walk down the aisle—the children have gone dead silent— and carry out my fantasy. The rest of the school day is bliss. For the first time in weeks I can actually hear my own voice above theirs.

The following morning when I arrive at Birkenhead Elementary the police and the head of the school are standing on the front steps waiting for me. I'm ushered into the principal's office and there face-down on the principal's desk, her dress up, her pink panties pulled down so the full bottom is exposed, is Lily Diamond. Her mother is there with her arms folded across her chest, the officers of the law are examining Lily Diamond's bottom and Lily is screaming.

"I told the American that caning is against the law in England," the head of the school says to the police.

"I had thought a cane was an actual cane," I say, product of the sixties, against all punishment, certainly corporal, now a sudden criminal in my own court.

"A cane is a cane," the head of the school says coolly.

The police make their assessment, give Lily a friendly slap.

"No mark appears to be evident," they say.

Lily hops off the desk, pulls up her pants, shakes herself proudly, giving me a look of complete disdain.

"Ain't you terrible sorry," she says, drawing the word to its full length.

5. It is the summer of my younger son's freshman year in high school and thirty boys are in our living room planning an insurrection. One among them, Danny C, has been dismissed, voted out by the faculty, flunked, they say, unable to return to the Quaker school for his sophomore year.

"How come?" I ask.

"He's an artist," my son says.

"They think he's weird."

"Different."

"Bad."

"Learning disabled." The new catchphrase.

I have known this boy since he was five—a curious, ebullient boy, neither athletic, nor in a conventional sense academic, imaginative, impulsive, fearless.

The boys are examining reasons for his dismissal, studying the school handbook that outlines the rules, looking over Danny's report cards that he has brought to the meeting, as well as the letters the school has sent to his parents that he has slipped out of his mother's file cabinet. They spend all day.

The rules are specific. No drugs, no alcohol, no cheating, no failing grades. There are twenty-six reasons for dismissal and Danny C, as the boys discover, hasn't measured up to any of them.

"Wear coats and ties," my husband says as the boys organize their defense for the head of the school.

The mothers of these boys cannot imagine a reversal of the faculty decision, but cheerleaders always, we drive them to school on the morning of their meeting with Mr. Harrison—thirty adolescent

boys with their argument in hand, point by point, all twenty-six reasons for dismissal addressed.

I wasn't at the meeting. The next I knew they were flooding into
the house, shedding their ties, a victorious army, organizing their
rule of the school for the next three years.

Mr. Harrison had reversed the decision.

"What happened?" I ask my son after everyone has gone home.

"Mr. Harrison is very brave," he says simply.

"How is that?" I ask.

"He listened to us."

6. When I am called to the nursery school where my oldest child is a
student, one of twelve in a class of two teachers, Mrs. Nice and Mrs.
Something Else, at the school where his father is head of the high
school, I have a new baby and a two-year-old and no baby-sitter, so
they come along. I have been called in to witness my son in action so
I will understand why these two women in a small class are unable to
manage him. So I sit in one of those little chairs with my finger in the
new baby's mouth so he won't cry and wait for the drama to unfold.

"Po," Mrs. Nice is talking. "Please sit down at the table and get
out your crayons."

No one else is sitting down but all around the room the other children turn to look at my son expectantly, a kind of pleasure in their
attitude, waiting for something to happen.

My son doesn't sit down.

"Po," Mrs. Nice says again. "What did I tell you?"

He puts his hands over his ears and walks around the periphery
of the room very quickly—dum dum dum dum de dum de dum de
dum de dum. His hands are in his pockets now and the other children are giggling at him, glancing back and forth at each other. He
gives them a knowing collaborator's look.

"You see?" Mrs. Nice says to me. She turns to my son as he passes
her on his march.

"Your mother is here watching, Po," she says as if this news will
come as a surprise to him. "So you better be good."

"He doesn't ever do what I ask him to do," Mrs. Nice says.

I am beginning to have that mother's sense of a temperature change in my son, an arriving decision, a moment of action. He has stopped his trip around the classroom and is listening to Mrs. Nice, an expression of bemusement on his face.

"Why haven't you told the other children to sit down?" I ask.

"Because they *will* sit down if I ask them to," she says. "So I don't need to ask them to, of course."

I am feeling homicidal.

Suddenly out of the corner of my eye, I see my son running across the room toward me, a maniacal smile on his face, leaping onto the table, racing around the edge of the circle with amazing speed and control, not even falling, his balance so perfect. All around the children are looking at him with something between admiration and envy.

Mrs. Nice is a picture of pure happiness.

"You see the problem, Mrs. Shreve?" she says. "Emotionally disturbed."

I pick up my two-year-old, grab Po by the hand, and we fly out of the room, down the corridor in which my four-year-old son spends hours sitting on a chair, into the parking lot, into the car and home.

"You see, Mom," Po says to me. "Mrs. Nice is crazy."

7. I am probably thirty-five, a teacher and administrator of an alternative school in Philadelphia called Our House for smart children in trouble, attending a conference of teachers in Atlanta where the major speaker will be Margaret Mead. I am sitting with my own children in the lobby of the hotel waiting for the speech when I notice a small, square woman, slightly hassled and bewildered, loaded down with bags and books and papers. I am in her line of vision and she stops.

"Do you know where the speech is?" she asks.

I know who this is, of course. These are the seventies, when Margaret Mead in many circles had the aura of a rock star. She was the mother of us all, accumulating weight from our acclamation.

I tell her this.

She is examining my children playing on the floor with Fisher-Price families and Legos and Matchbox cars.

"Are you coming to the speech?"

"Yes, I am," I reply, adding some compliment that she ignores.

"My speech is about the end of the family as we know it," she looks at me, assessing my role as mother. "Parents have abdicated their role and now the school must take over the family's job. In the next twenty years, they won't have time to educate." She brushes her small hands together, walks between a plastic Fisher-Price family and heads to the lectern.

8. I sit down in the office of the college guidance counselor, relieved that for the fourth and last time I am about to set out on the trip to look at colleges for a child. Especially with this child, this reader of *Anna Karenina* who has told me that she would prefer to be homeschooled or else to go to a fiercely strict Catholic school with nuns who carry rulers peering out of stiff white boards. Either freedom or confinement is what she's after. Not this wishy-washy middle of accommodation and concern and judgment, because no choice a child could possibly make in this atmosphere of freedom of choice will be the right one.

The college guidance counselor and my daughter are already seated and there is decision about the room.

"We are meeting to talk about Kate's college choices, which she should make by the end of her junior year," the counselor says.

Kate has been a good student in spite of her limited attendance, so I'm not worried, in fact almost comfortable this fourth time around.

"So what are you thinking, Kate?" the counselor asks, a conversation I can tell they have already had and are repeating for my benefit.

"I'm actually leaving high school," Kate says.

The counselor, a Quaker and therefore by definition nonconfrontational, looks at me with something close to fury.

"We have never had a student choose to drop out of high school in her junior year," she says.

"I didn't know this was happening," I say, immediately sorry that

I hadn't said instead: "Of course. Kate and I discussed the subject last night and decided that high school was absolutely useless for her. Many better things to do with her time."

"I'm very sorry," Kate says, and always polite adds that she is quite fond of the school, admiring of the college counselor, respectful of the values, but simply is no longer willing to spend her time there.

In the car coming home, trying to concentrate in order not to run a stop sign or red light or hyperventilate, I ask Kate what she plans to do.

"I haven't decided," she says. "I simply know that I'm not suited to high school."

I am reminded of a conversation I overheard when as a young mother I went to visit a friend whose daughter was in high school.

We were sitting in the living room when her daughter came home from school, dropped her books, her coat, and flopped down on the couch.

"I am miserable in high school," she said crossly to her mother.

"I'm so glad to hear that, darling," my friend said cheerfully. "All of the interesting people I know were miserable in high school."

9. Elizabeth is in fourth grade at a new school and I imagine that she's perfectly happy, since that's what she tells me. She is making new friends, although she doesn't want them to come over and never seems to be invited to their houses. She only misses her old school at night when I turn out the light in her room. So it comes as a terrible surprise when one of the fourth grade mothers asks me do I know about the I Hate Elizabeth Club. The mother has just discovered that her daughter belongs to it. Membership in the club costs a dollar, she tells me, and all of the girls in the fourth grade have been asked to join or else to suffer exclusion if they refuse. The rules are simple. No one is allowed to speak to Elizabeth and members are rewarded for an imaginative punishment such as the sticking of straight pins in my daughter's back during Meeting for Worship.

"I thought it was my fault," Elizabeth says when I ask her why she never told me. She doesn't cry. She begs me not to tell the teacher or it will be worse for her.

"I have to," I tell her. "What they have done is terrible and your teacher has to know about it. She's in charge."

That night she tells me everything. Day after miserable day of the I Hate Elizabeth Club while I in my stupidity was thinking she was happy.

"What are you going to do to them?" she asks, lying next to me in the dark.

I have made a decision. Already what was done to my child is forming itself into a story in my mind.

"I'm going to write a book about them and call them each by name," I say.

"Maybe you'll be sued," she says.

"I won't be sued," I reply.

Sometime later, maybe three years, I am at lunch with Elizabeth and the former president of the I Hate Elizabeth Club. They aren't friends of course but the former president is trying. I can tell she wants to tell me something, has thought about it for a long time. She has apologized to Elizabeth, once when she had to because she was caught, and recently, just weeks before, when she meant it.

"You used my real name," she says finally.

"Yes I did."

"I read the book," she says. "I didn't realize what I'd done until I read about myself."

One of the accomplishments of this collection of essays and stories by writers many of whom have also become teachers is to illustrate the value of difference, to honor the importance of connection, to show the way in which a story reminds us what it is like to be a child in case we have forgotten. At the heart of teaching is not content but a recognition of the child as an individual. Those few teachers who *know* us when we are young go the full distance in our internal lives. It is not an easy task. What good teachers finally do is make things right for the line of children behind their own childhood and, like the writers in this collection, they remember their own tales out of school.

SHERMAN ALEXIE

Indian Education

FIRST GRADE

My hair was too short and my U.S. Government glasses were horn-rimmed, ugly, and all that first winter in school, the other Indian boys chased me from one corner of the playground to the other. They pushed me down, buried me in the snow until I couldn't breathe, thought I'd never breathe again.

They stole my glasses and threw them over my head, around my outstretched hands, just beyond my reach, until someone tripped me and sent me falling again, facedown in the snow.

I was always falling down; my Indian name was Junior Falls Down. Sometimes it was Bloody Nose or Steal-His-Lunch. Once, it was Cries-Like-a-White-Boy, even though none of us had seen a white boy cry.

Then it was a Friday morning recess and Frenchy SiJohn threw snowballs at me while the rest of the Indian boys tortured some other *top-yogh-yaught* kid, another weakling. But Frenchy was confident enough to torment me all by himself, and most days I would have let him.

But the little warrior in me roared to life that day and knocked Frenchy to the ground, held his head against the snow, and punched him so hard that my knuckles and the snow made symmetrical bruises on his face. He almost looked like he was wearing war paint.

But he wasn't the warrior. I was. And I chanted *It's a good day to die, it's a good day to die,* all the way down to the principal's office.

SECOND GRADE

Betty Towle, missionary teacher, redheaded and so ugly that no one ever had a puppy crush on her, made me stay in for recess fourteen days straight.

"Tell me you're sorry," she said.

"Sorry for what?" I asked.

"Everything," she said and made me stand straight for fifteen minutes, eagle-armed with books in each hand. One was a math book; the other was English. But all I learned was that gravity can be painful.

For Halloween I drew a picture of her riding a broom with a scrawny cat on the back. She said that her God would never forgive me for that.

Once, she gave the class a spelling test but set me aside and gave me a test designed for junior high students. When I spelled all the words right, she crumpled up the paper and made me eat it.

"You'll learn respect," she said.

She sent a letter home with me that told my parents to either cut by braids or keep me home from class. My parents came in the next day and dragged their braids across Betty Towle's desk.

"Indians, indians, indians." She said it without capitalization. She called me "indian, indian, indian."

And I said, *Yes, I am. I am Indian. Indian, I am.*

THIRD GRADE

My traditional Native American art career began and ended with my very first portrait: *Stick Indian Taking a Piss in My Backyard.*

As I circulated the original print around the classroom, Mrs. Schluter intercepted and confiscated my art.

Censorship, I might cry now. *Freedom of expression,* I would write in editorials to the tribal newspaper.

In third grade, though, I stood alone in the corner, faced the wall, and waited for the punishment to end.

I'm still waiting.

FOURTH GRADE

"You should be a doctor when you grow up," Mr. Schluter told me, even though his wife, the third grade teacher, thought I was crazy beyond my years. My eyes always looked like I had just hit-and-run someone.

"Guilty," she said. "You always look guilty."

"Why should I be a doctor?" I asked Mr. Schluter.

"So you can come back and help the tribe. So you can heal people."

That was the year my father drank a gallon of vodka a day and the same year that my mother started two hundred different quilts but never finished any. They sat in separate, dark places in our HUD house and wept savagely.

I ran home after school, heard their Indian tears, and looked in the mirror. *Doctor Victor,* I called myself, invented an education, talked to my reflection. *Doctor Victor to the emergency room.*

FIFTH GRADE

I picked up a basketball for the first time and made my first shot. No. I missed my first shot, missed the basket completely, and the ball landed in the dirt and sawdust, sat there just like I had sat there only minutes before.

But it felt good, that ball in my hands, all those possibilities and angles. It was mathematics, geometry. It was beautiful.

At that same moment, my cousin Steven Ford sniffed rubber cement from a paper bag and leaned back on the merry-go-round. His ears rang, his mouth was dry, and everyone seemed so far away.

But it felt good, that buzz in his head, all those colors and noises. It was chemistry, biology. It was beautiful.

Oh, do you remember those sweet, almost innocent choices that the Indian boys were forced to make?

SIXTH GRADE

Randy, the new Indian kid from the white town of Springdale, got into a fight an hour after he first walked into the reservation school.

Stevie Flett called him out, called him a squawman, called him a pussy, and called him a punk.

Randy and Stevie, and the rest of the Indian boys, walked out into the playground.

"Throw the first punch," Stevie said as they squared off.

"No," Randy said.

"Throw the first punch," Stevie said again.

"No," Randy said again.

"Throw the first punch!" Stevie said for the third time, and Randy reared back and pitched a knuckle fastball that broke Stevie's nose.

We all stood there in silence, in awe.

That was Randy, my soon-to-be first and best friend, who taught me the most valuable lesson about living in the white world: *Always throw the first punch.*

SEVENTH GRADE

I leaned through the basement window of the HUD house and kissed the white girl who would later be raped by her foster-parent father, who was also white. They both lived on the reservation, though, and when the headlines and stories filled the papers later, not one word was made of their color.

Just Indians being Indians, someone must have said somewhere and they were wrong.

But on the day I leaned through the basement window of the

HUD house and kissed the white girl, I felt the good-byes I was saying to my entire tribe. I held my lips tight against her lips, a dry, clumsy, and ultimately stupid kiss.

But I was saying good-bye to my tribe, to all the Indian girls and women I might have loved, to all the Indian men who might have called me cousin, even brother.

I kissed that white girl and when I opened my eyes, she was gone from the reservation, and when I opened my eyes, I was gone from the reservation, living in a farm town where a beautiful white girl asked my name.

"Junior Polatkin," I said, and she laughed.

After that, no one spoke to me for another five hundred years.

EIGHTH GRADE

At the farm town junior high, in the boys' bathroom, I could hear voices from the girls' bathroom, nervous whispers of anorexia and bulimia. I could hear the white girls' forced vomiting, a sound so familiar and natural to me after years of listening to my father's hangovers.

"Give me your lunch if you're just going to throw it up," I said to one of those girls once.

I sat back and watched them grow skinny from self-pity.

Back on the reservation, my mother stood in line to get us commodities. We carried them home, happy to have food, and opened the canned beef that even the dogs wouldn't eat.

But we ate it day after day and grew skinny from self-pity.

There is more than one way to starve.

NINTH GRADE

At the farm town high school dance, after a basketball game in an overheated gym where I had scored twenty-seven points and pulled down thirteen rebounds, I passed out during a slow song.

As my white friends revived me and prepared to take me to the emergency room where doctors would later diagnose my diabetes, the Chicano teacher ran up to us.

"Hey," he said. "What's that boy been drinking? I know all about these Indian kids. They start drinking real young."

Sharing dark skin doesn't necessarily make two men brothers.

TENTH GRADE

I passed the written test easily and nearly flunked the driving, but still received my Washington State driver's license on the same day that Wally Jim killed himself by driving his car into a pine tree.

No traces of alcohol in his blood, good job, wife and two kids.

"Why'd he do it?" asked a white Washington State trooper.

All the Indians shrugged their shoulders, looked down at the ground.

"Don't know," we all said, but when we look in the mirror, see the history of our tribe in our eyes, taste failure in the tap water, and shake with old tears, we understand completely.

Believe me, everything looks like a noose if you stare at it long enough.

ELEVENTH GRADE

Last night I missed two free throws which would have won the game against the best team in the state. The farm town high school I play for is nicknamed the "Indians," and I'm probably the only actual Indian ever to play for a team with such a mascot.

This morning I pick up the sports page and read the headline: INDIANS LOSE AGAIN.

Go ahead and tell me none of this is supposed to hurt me very much.

TWELFTH GRADE

I walk down the aisle, valedictorian of this farm town high school, and my cap doesn't fit because I've grown my hair longer than it's ever been. Later, I stand as the school board chairman recites my awards, accomplishments, and scholarships.

I try to remain stoic for the photographers as I look toward the future.

Back home on the reservation, my former classmates graduate: a few can't read, one or two are just given attendance diplomas, most look forward to the parties. The bright students are shaken, frightened, because they don't know what comes next.

They smile for the photographer as they look back toward tradition.

The tribal newspaper runs my photograph and the photograph of my former classmates side by side.

POSTSCRIPT: CLASS REUNION

Victor said, "Why should we organize a reservation high school reunion? My graduating class has a reunion every weekend at the Pow-wow Tavern."

STUART DYBEK

Field Trips

We took two field trips in grade school. The first was a tour of the Bridewell House of Corrections and the Cook County Jail. The prison complex was on twenty-sixth and California, only blocks away from St. Roman's School, so, herded by nuns into an orderly column with the girls in front and boys bringing up the rear, our fifth grade class walked there. The nuns must have thought it a perfect choice for a field trip as not only was there a suitable cautionary lesson, but it saved on bus fare, too.

Filing from school at midmorning felt like a jailbreak. Paired up with pals, we traipsed down California, gaping like tourists at the familiar street coming to life—delivery trucks double-parking before greasy spoons, open doors revealing the dark interiors of bars still exhaling boozy breath from the night before. Some of the kids like Bad Brad Norky—already twice convicted of stealing the class milk money—were hoping to see various relatives who were doing time at County. Others, like my best friend, Rafael Mendoza, were hoping to catch a glimpse of a mob boss, or a mass murderer, or the infamous psychopath Edward Gein, a farmer from the wilds of Illinois who supposedly cannibalized his victims and tanned their skins to make lampshades and clothes. Gein fascinated us. Some years later when I was in high school, I bought a pair of hand-stitched moccasin-top gray suede shoes that when soaked with rain turned a cadaverous shade, and my buddies took to calling them my Gein shoes. That, in turn, developed into a neighborhood expression of appreciation for any article of clothing that looked sharp in an unconventional way: *muy Gein, man,* or *Gein cool!* At the same time, the term could also be used as an insult: "Your mama's a Gein."

Even more than the murderers and celebrity psychos, the main draw at County, at least for the boys, was getting a look at the electric chair. We'd heard it was kept in the basement. Local legend had it that a sudden burst of static on the radio or a blink in TV reception, say, during the *Howdy Doody* show, meant that the power had surged because they'd just fried someone at County. We thought maybe we'd get to shake the hand of the warden or whoever flipped the switch at executions. But, if there was an electric chair there at all, we never got to see it.

Surprisingly, the most memorable part of the trip occurred not at County where the men, penned in what the tour guide informed us were sixty-square-foot cells, mostly ignored us, but rather at Bridewell when they took us through the women's wing. The inmates there, prostitutes mainly, saw the nuns and had some comments about being Brides of Christ that were truly educational:

"Yo, Sisters, what kinda meat do the pope eat on Friday? Nun."

"Hey, Sister Mary Hymen, when I dress up like that I get an extra fifty!"

The nuns didn't respond, but their faces assumed the same impassive, inwardly suffering expressions that the statues of martyrs wore, and they began to hurry us through the rest of the tour.

A hefty female guard rapped the bars with her stick and shouted, "Pipe down, Taffy, there's kids for godssake."

And Taffy laughed, "Shee-it, Bull Moose! When I was their age I was doing my daddy."

And from another cell someone called, "Amen, girl!"

The next year the nuns avoided the jail and instead took us to the stockyards, a trip that required a bus. A rented yellow school bus was already waiting when we got to school that morning, and we filed on, boys sitting on the left side of the aisle, girls on the right. I sat next to a new kid, Joseph Bonnamo. Usually, new kids were quiet and with-drawn, but Bonnamo who'd only been at St. Roman's for a couple weeks was already the most popular boy in the class. Everyone called him Joey B. His father had been a marine lifer and Joey B was used to moving around, he said. He'd moved around so much that he was a grade behind, a year older than everyone else, but he didn't seem ashamed by it. He was a good athlete and the girls all had crushes on him. That included Sylvie Perez, who over the summer had sud-denly, to use my mother's word, "developed." Exploded into bloom was closer to the truth. Along with the rest of the boys, I pretended as best I could not to notice—it was too intimidating to those of us who'd been her classmates for years. But not to Joey B.

"Like my old man says, 'Tits that size have a mind of their own,'" he confided to me on the way to the Yards, "and hers are thinking 'Feel me up, Joey B.'"

"How do you know?"

His hand dropped down and he clutched his crotch. "Telepathy."

"Class," Sister Bull Moose asked, "do you know our tradition when riding a bus on a field trip?"

"A round pound?" Joey B whispered to me.

No one raised a hand. We didn't know we had a tradition—as far as we knew we were the first class from St. Roman's ever to take a bus on a field trip.

Sister Bull Moose's real name was Sister Amabilia, but she had a heft to her that meant business, and she wielded the baton she used to conduct choir practice not unlike the guard we'd seen wielding a nightstick at Bridewell a year before, so my friend Rafael had come up with the nickname.

From within her habit, a garment that looked as if it had infinite storage capacity, she produced the pitch pipe also used in choir prac-tice and sustained a note. "Girls start and boys come in on 'Merrily merrily merrily . . .'"

Joey B sang in my ear, "Row row row your boner . . ."

At the Yards there was a regular tour. First stop was the Armour pack-ing plant where the meat was processed into bacon and sausage. I think the entire class was relieved that the smell wasn't as bad as we worried it might be. We knew we had traveled to the source of what in the neighborhood was called "the brown wind" or "the glue pee-ew factory," a stench that settled over the south side of Chicago at least once a week. My father said it was the smell of boiling hooves, hair, and bone rendered down to make soap. I'd once dissected a bar of Ivory on which I'd noticed what appeared to be animal hair to see if there were also fragments of bone and if beneath the soap smell I could detect the reek of the Yards.

We left the processing plant for the slaughterhouse and from a metal catwalk looked upon the scene below where workmen wearing yellow hard hats and white coats smeared with gore heaved sledge hammers down on the skulls of the steers that, urged by electric prods, had filed obediently through wooden chutes.

Every time the hammer connected, my friend Rafael would go, "Ka-boom!"

The steer would drop, folding at the knees as if his front legs had suddenly been broken.

"That has to smart," Joey B said.

For the finale they took us to where the hogs were slaughtered. A man with hairy, thick, spattered forearms, wearing rubber boots and a black rubber apron shiny with blood, stood holding a butcher knife before a vat of water. An assembly line of huge squealing hogs, suspended by their hind legs, swung past him, and as each hog went by the line would pause long enough for the man to slit the hog's throat. He did it with a practiced, effortless motion and I wondered how long he'd had the job, what it had been like on his first day, and if it was a job I could ever be desperate enough to do. Up to then, my idea of the worst job one could have was bus driver. I didn't think I could drive through rush-hour traffic down the same street over and over while making change as bus drivers had to in those days. But watching the man kill hogs, I began to think that driving a bus might not be so bad.

With each hog there was the same terrified squeal, but louder than a squeal, more like a shriek that became a grunting gurgle of blood. A Niagara of blood splashed to the tile and into a flowing gut-ter of water where it rushed frothing away. The man would plunge the knife into the vat of water before him and the water clouded pink, then he'd withdraw the shining blade just as the next squealing hog arrived. Meanwhile, the hogs who'd just cranked by, still alive, their mouths, nostrils, and slit throats pumping dark red gouts were swung into a bundle of hanging bodies to bleed. Each new carcass slammed into the others causing a few weak squeals and a fresh gush of blood.

The tour guide apologized that we couldn't see the sheep slaughtered. He said that some people thought the sheep sounded human, like children, and that bothered some people, so they didn't include it on the tour.

It made me wonder who killed the sheep. We'd seen the men with sledgehammers and the man with a knife. How were the sheep slaughtered? Was it a promotion to work with the sheep—some place they sent only the most expert slaughterers—or was it the job that nobody at the Yards wanted?

"Just like the goddamn electric chair," Rafael complained.

"How's that?" Joey B asked.

"They wouldn't let us see the chair when we went to the jail last year."

At the end of the tour on our way out of the processing plant they gave each of us a souvenir hot dog. Not a hot dog Chicago style: poppy seed bun, mustard—never catsup, onion, relish, tomato, pickle, peppers, celery salt. This was a cold hot dog wrapped in a napkin. We hadn't had lunch and everyone was starving. We rode back on the bus eating our hot dogs, while singing "Frère Jacques."

I was sitting by the window, Joey B beside me, and right across the aisle from him—no accident, probably—was Sylvie Perez. I realized it was a great opportunity, but I could never think of anything to say to girls in a situation like that.

"Sylvie," Joey B said, "you liking that hot dog?"

"It's okay," Sylvie said.

"You look good eating it," he told her.

It sounded like the stupidest thing I'd ever heard, but all she did was blush, smile at him, and take another demure nibble.

I knew it was against the rules, but I cracked open the window of the bus and tried to flick my balled-up hot dog napkin into a passing convertible. Sister Bull Moose saw me do it.

"Why does there always have to be one who's not mature enough to take on trips," she asked rhetorically. For punishment I had to give up my seat and stand in the aisle, which I did to an indifference on the part of Sylvie Perez that was the worst kind of scorn.

"Since you obviously need special attention, Stuart, you can sing us a round," Sister said. Once, during our weekly music hour, looking in my direction, she'd inquired, "Who is singing like an off-key foghorn?" When I'd shut up, still moving my mouth, but only pretending to sing, she'd said, "That's better."

"I don't know the words," I said.

"Oh, I think you do. *'Dor-mez-vous, dor-mez-vous, Bim Bam Boon.'* They're easy."

Joey B patted the now empty seat beside him as if to say to Sylvie, "Now you can sit here."

Sylvie rolled her pretty eyes toward Sister Bull Moose and smiled, and Joey B nodded he understood and smiled back, and they rode like that in silence, communicating telepathically while I sang.

CAROLYN FERRELL

Tiger-Frame Glasses

The squad was made up of three girls from a school. The girls names was Debbie, Donna, and Shenay. They was stalwart, steady, and statuesque, always going round not hurting old people or weak boys but helping them. They strolled down Ronald Drive and Cahill Street to Nathalie Avenue to way over to Jefferson Estates, where they could be invited in some Body's house for cookies and where they could automatically spot trouble. Things that needed correcting. A yelling mother. A father that liked to observe things too much. A brother that was in danger of getting left back in school with a bunch of stupids. A sister that didn't have no friends and was going to get murderized by some others and furthermore she thought she was going crazy. For instance. That was at day.

At night they came together and decided Who Should Benefit From Our Good Deeds? They all had Good Hearts. They was all big strong girl students that did science superbly smart and got into the honor roll just from their math grade. You Know Girls Can Be Boy Smart. The Helper Squad was loved by every Body in Amity-ville. They was a home for girls and boys that had secrets and that needed things corrected. The Helper Squad mothers and fathers wanted the girls to be stupendous.

(That's how I made them in my notebook. Stupendous.)

Their mothers and fathers let them talk about babies and how babies came, just as long as they don't have none of their own. Right now you all

14

just help and do right. We love you just like you are. And don't forget: You
are the Ones.

(That's how I made them.)

They had us in a circle of two, all by ourself, them close to where the
bus comes, me and Bethi in a circle by ourself, but then they broke it
up by telling Bethi that I had called her a slow girl in Mr. di Salvo's
class yesterday so then I was an only circle. They told her Come Stand
Over Here By Us. Bethi looked at me with her mouth hanging open,
nothing new. She went over to the back opening of their circle. Then
it was just me to make a circle out of one person, waiting for the bus
which would surely include more agony. Bethi and I were apart, but
together by radar we were waiting to get to Park Avenue Elementary
and by radar remembering when my head got massacred in a fusil-
lade of blood by Bibi and Crater and Martha and Bellerina last summer on this very corner. We listened to their ugly brains and their
ugly ways. I wanted them like my whole Body was fire.

—I'm going with Charlie to the Back. I am his world.

—What you doing there? No one is suppose to be in the Back.

—None of your fucking business.

—The Back is where the lezzies go. You a homo.

—Teeny, tell your sister she's butt-ugly. You cunnylingling.

—What's that mean?

—Look in the mirror.

—No one is suppose to be in the Back. They say that's where girls.

—Look in the mirror.

They would giggle like monsters and it would fill in all the air that I
had saved up in my head. I was trying to be self-independent and
breathe my own air. My notebook was in my bag with all my stories
in it and was my own air. I had learned about Indians in the Nine-
teenth Century being self-independent, especially when the Fron-
tiersmen had it out with them over all the harms they were causing.
The wagon trains moved in a circle and pulled out shotguns under
the flaps. The Pioneers suffered. They had a dream. That one day this

nation will rise up. The Pioneer People built America because they would not let their dream get stoppled. I learned from Mr. di Salvo that the Indians could be awful quiet, holding in their breath in the shrubberies when ambush was near. The Pioneer People would be sitting in the wagon train with women and children, some who could read and write. But they could not make out the thunder in the ground or the smoke signals from the rocks that said: You was born to sacrifice for this great land.

I do the same in my circle.

Ass. Asshole. Cunny. Four Eye Fuck. Think You a Brainiac, but You is a fucking Re-Tard. You and Your Fucking Notebook Full of Lies. (Why you have to write lies like that?) You and You Re-Tard Sister. I'ma Kick Your Goddamn Ass. Like I did Last Summer Remember. You better stay indoors. WITH YOUR NOTEBOOK. Slow Girl will be a Dead Girl. Yeah I'm Looking at You. Four Eye Fuck.

The other girls giggle gigantic giggles. Then Bellerina's sister Gimlet and her girl *friend* Big Susie come by on their way to high school and just stand there, letting the girls look them up and down. Every Body drinks in Gimlet and Big Susie and knows in their heart that they are the rulers, even if no Body is allowed to say what else they are. Bethi is just standing there not doing a thing. Because it wasn't *her* head that got massacred last summer, the braids all torn up, the teeth in shatters. The eyes in a clump. No writing hand at all. All because of the notebook I keep with the stories. Only the girls from the bus stop think it was all about them which it was not. Bethi doesn't know what she is doing there in the girls circle. I make a note to myself that I will have to explain that to her later on. That and a thousand other things like how to be good friends with the teachers. The ones that can still be outraged and feel for you.

I watch their mouths. I try to listen with my eyes close. I can see Gimlet yanking her sister Bellerina by the hair telling her You Better not be Doing It, then lighting up a cigarette in front of every Body and then passing it to Big Susie who runs her tongue along the cigarette before she takes it in her lips and smiles back at Gimlet. From where I am standing, the girls mouths move to things that don't make any sense, like Teeny's mouth saying over and over, I want visitor hands of cyclone skirt, I want visitor hands of cyclone skirt. Every Body laughs. Which shrinks my only girl circle. Gimlet looks over in my direction but she don't do anything. Big Susie says, Yall ain't supposed to play like that. That supposed to be your fren! Only she knows it ain't playing. Something will happen that will get my ass kicked again. The other girl circle wants me in-tense. Gimlet puts her hand in Big Susie's jeans behind pocket and she and her keep on walking to the high school. I hold my breath. We watch till they're a speck. I turn my eyes down. I feel what they want. Out under the new tiger-frame glasses I'm wearing there is a world of uncovered things like hands, hair, voices, teeth, windows, behinds, desires.

(They were the most perfect girls I could think of.)

Debbie, Virgo, her favorite color was red, like the setting sun over the mountains you could see from her bedroom window. She was precise, innocent, shy, perfectionist, of service to others. Solicitous. The time she wanted to go with Donna's brother's best friend but her good virtuous held her down. All the times she got a 100 grade in math class, but she didn't say nothing. She was modesty carnation.

Donna was in love with her brother's best friend. He loved her back although he was secretly more in love with Debbie. But there are some bonds and some promises that are stronger than the Heart Dictation. There is Honor. There is Friendship. There is another Girl Truth.

Donna, Aries, was a grade A student and the most beautiful girl in the school. Sometimes rash, sometimes thorny, but always up front. Everyone wanted to say that Cynthia Wiggins was the most beautiful, but secretly they knew that beauty is not just outwardly. No, what about all that on the inside? And Donna's biggest wish in life was to become a veterinarian and take care of sick injured horses.

At the Divine Confabulation Private School For Girls Donna asked to play a slave in the Thanksgiving Assembly in the fifth grade. Everyone wanted to be a Mistress on a plantation, but Donna knew right from wrong. She was her mother and father pride and joy. Her favorite colors was brown and white.

*   *   *

In school Mr. di Salvo asks me if I can spell the word appreciate. If I can spell it correctly, I will get to be one of the Women in the Pioneer play. I will get to sing "This Land Is Your Land" with the other Women. I will get to have Mrs. Shea from third grade sew me a bonnet and a long apron to wear over my clothes when I walk along the stage with the others. All this for appreciate on our weekly spelling bee. Bellerina sees that I am having trouble. She and I are at the middle desk. She has not had her hair braided in days. There are all these little nubs down the back of her neck. The Ultra-Sheen grease that her mother told her to put in missed her hair and smacks down her neck and shows my reflection in it. I can almost see my corduroy pants on her neck through my tiger-frame glasses that everyone makes fun of and calls me F.E.F. cause they know I won't do nothing. I only have one pair of pants. My parents say that we are poor, but not to go out broadcasting that information. How can I help it? My knees are run down. Every Body knows. And I can't do nothing. But the school bus on page 2 of the spelling book honks to me: appreciate, appreciate. The Boloney Butcher for B whispers, I *appreciate* a truly smart girl like you. I am going stark raving for a girl in the fifth grade who is going to get it later on from the girls at the bus stop. A whole bunch of dreams. I want to do something. Will my parents finally go away with us on vacation to the mountains or the seaside like they promised? Will they send me and Bethi to private school—where we *really* belong? A truly smart girl. My brain remembers the melody lane from the day before in the backyard: Daddy mowing the dried up lawn and whistling "California Dreamer" and Mom singing the commercial for Eight O'Clock Coffee and Bethi trying to get all the words to "Shakeit Shakeit Shakeit" in one line, like there are no other words to the whole song. Me sitting in the bushes with my notebook which is the dream weavill and trying to get it all down the way I would truly like it to happen and looking up in the sunlight and wishing I had a real mother and a real father and a real sister that wanted the utmost best for me, who realized all the dynamite I have in me, like a princess or a very smart and beautiful princess/girl/student. I listen. I want to shout to Bethi, "We're going to the country,

We're going to the fair" as those are the other words, but she is really too slow to get anything. I hate her.

Bellerina whispers in my ear A-P-P-R-E-S-H-E-A-T-E. I repeat her words. I want to stand in the girls circle. When I *used* to be there, Bellerina used to play the funniest jokes on me, and I wouldn't get mad. She had told Bibi in secret exactly *where* it would hurt the most on my Body to hit me, and she was right. She told my notebook to see the stories I wrote in it so she could give the others more ammunition. She informed me that she would get her older brother Beanie from prison to take me to the Back and feel my nubs under my dress. She did all this and still. I want to stand in the girls circle. I will spin Bethi out, cause she really don't know what it means, the circle. She don't know that I should have what she has, only she don't recognize that for her genuine slowness.

Mr. di Salvo announces that I will be one of the people pulling the wagon across the prairie. They had those too, you know, when the horses died, and the cattle broke down. I don't have to wear a dress if I don't want to. The girls wearing aprons and bonnets will have to wear a dress under. But I can wear whatever I want to, even my gym suit, as a puller.

The songs I will have to sing with the chorus are "Fifty Miles on the Erie Canal." "Sweet Betsy from Pike." "Carry My Back to Ole Virginny." I will have to walk slow like they did in the old days. They did not run across the prairie. I will have to learn my songs good. Bellerina holds her big teeth under her big hand. She will get to be a Pioneer Woman. She will get a bonnet and an apron. She will get to sit in the wagon while the boys and some unlucky girls pull it. Even though she weighs as much as a ninth-grader one ton and she is butt-ugly.

The teacher is not expecting nothing. I was born on Easter, an Aries baby, so that makes me the kind that is innocent yet secretly commanding. I raise my hand and I get up slowly out my desk. My palms are sweaty. My long braids that I hate for my mother to make on me are messed up already because I've been putting my head down on my boring speller too much. I get up. The gray venetian blinds on the big window hold back the sun with their straight arms and tell me that I am in the right lane. Go on Girlie, they cheer! They reach down and pat my head like I'm the faithful dog. The door frame gets ready to move. The tiles on the floor are shivery with delight. Shakeit Shakeit Shakeit. Shakeit all you can. I open my mouth. "Bellerina Brown is a Fucking Ass. Hole." The class goes wild. Shakeit all you can. Shakeit like a milk-shake, and do the best you can. The venetian blinds nod yes you can and the clouds outside fall into the classroom and swirl my brains up in a pudding. Bellerina swings for my stomach, but I land on Mr. di Salvo's desk, where I hide with the other butterflies under the stack of math tests from last Wednesday. A staunch stunning wind from the spelling lists stampedes the stalactites on my hands. Bellerina punches but I am too fast. I'm always out her way.

With both eyes open under my tiger-frame glasses I see the pretty *one hundred* girls who are in shock and who don't want to consider me anymore for them. The rough *zero* girls have questions for me later: *we ain't know you was like us, Glory!* The snaggle tooth boys cheer Hip Hip, and Boo-Boo claps me on the back. Mr. di Salvo takes me and Bellerina out the play. We will have to sit in Mrs. Shea's class with the third-graders while the assembly is on. We will have to write out the words to "The Star Spangled Banner" ten times and maybe get locked in the closet, which is Mrs. Shea's specialty.

Bellerina looks me up and down.—Later, Today, After-school. Your Ass is Grass.

I sit back in my seat. The pencil groove on my desk smiles and asks me, Now that wasn't so hard, was it?

(The story goes on.)

Shenay is a Scorpio. She do not bother with boys at all. She is sexy, strategic and silent. She figures things out. Shenay has one mission on her mind: Find those who need help, and send in the Helper Squad. That would be her, Donna and Debbie. They all live on the same street and at night, they are all dedicated to saving.

Shenay can open her bedroom window and get the feel of the ocean waves crashing against the rock. She teaches Donna and Debbie. She tells them to look behind what you see. Look for the genuine-ality of a thing. Donna and Debbie say I don't get it. Shenay says, "Let me give you an example."

When she is lying in her bed at night, she sees gypsy moths fistfighting in the wall and hears pumpernickel swans discussing yesterday's math problems together. Did you get this one? Sure. That one was a cinch. The swans kiss her on the forehead. Honey, you ain't never told us you were such a smartie.

Shenay says, "Look."

On my way to the principal's office to get my punishment okayed I pass Bethi's classroom and wave to the teacher, Mr. Flegenheimer. Can she come out right now? I just got an important message from our mother and I just want to tell her it in the hall, Mr. Fleg. Private. It's important from our mother.

Mr. Flegenheimer brings Bethi out because he is getting too many complaints from the parents of special ed that he is not treating their kids like regular human beings. That he is holding back their bathroom and making them pee in their chairs and sit in it for a long time before calling the nurse and the janitor. That he is closing the venetian blinds and making them sit there, just like that, so he can put his head down on the desk. Mr. Flegenheimer is trying to look different now, but we all know.

—You can talk for three minutes, and I mean three minutes, Glory. I have a good mind to talk to your mother on the phone to confirm this, Mr. Flegenheimer says. Then he is gone back to the class that is howling over something. His eyes are closed.

Bethi is afraid to look at me. She just got allowed into the back of their circle this morning. She is afraid of what I will do to her. Don't worry about that till later, I assure her. I will get you back later. Right now I want you to do me a favor. I want you to go to Mr. di Salvo's classroom and tell him to send Bellerina to your classroom, Mr. Flegenheimer's orders. Can you do that? Okay Bethi? Can you do that? I whisper all this to her, but it takes a real long time before she gets the directions straight. She is not a retard. She is just slow. Her whole classroom is full of slow kids, so she don't feel so alone. They get beat up all the time, except for the large ones that are truly brainless and that can kill you just by looking your way.

Bethi goes to my classroom and gets Bellerina who calls her Stupid Ass and Brick Brain all the way back to Mr. Flegenheimer's door. I'm waiting there. Martha Madison suddenly appears out of nowhere humming her group of Women's song for Assembly "I'se Gwine Back to Dixie." She says in my direction, You Gonna Wish You Was Dead Meat. Martha is cross-eyed so she sometimes scares me and she sometimes doesn't. Now I am only thinking of my plan. Bellerina slaps her five and then Martha books. Bellerina turns and looks me dead in the eye. There, I am there. Shakeit Shakeit.

The door opened to show the first victim in need: old Mrs. Goodwin, a faithful soul who had a heart of gold. She was a white lady who trusted everyone. She lived all by herself in the black neighborhood of Tar Hill where people live in apartments instead of normal houses. She can make you believe in mankind all over again. Hallelujah for Mrs. Goodwin!

She had fell down her apartment steps and all the food stamp cans of food in her grocery bag rolled into the alleyway where Joe the town bum was laying. "Help me Joe!" she cried, but he only cried back, "Mrs. Goodwin, indeed I wish I could! I myself am too weak to do much of anything." So they both agonized in tribulations until around the corner came—the Helper Squad!

Debbie helped the old bitty to her feet, but when she found that Mrs. Goodwin couldn't walk, she carried her in her girl arms up the steps to her house and put her in the bed. Donna said, "Debbie, how come you got so strong?" Debbie didn't want to say. Modesty carnation.

Donna placed all the cans of food in their cabinets and to top it off, she cooked Mrs. Goodwin a whole dinner. Saucy Frank Supper with corn and tomatoes in it. Mrs. Goodwin closed her wrinkly eyes with tears of joy. "What would this world be without girls like you?" Donna shaked her beautiful hair and made Mrs. Goodwin feel better just by looking at her.

Meanwhile Shenay was in the alleyway helping Joe the bum to his feet. He smelled strange and warm. She was telling him, "See, if you believe in yourself, you can do it." Joe said he had never believed in himself

before today. He was going downtown to get a job at the local school, do-
ing anything. He wants to better himself. Maybe he can raise to a janitor.
Shenay, you are a gold mind. *Let me* thank *you.*

"*Don't thank me. Thank the Helper Squad. We want the world to be*
the place where you can dream and come true."

"*I* need *to thank you, Shenay.*"

"*I said* don't, *old man.*"

Back then. The daylights whipped out of me. I said I couldn't take it
no more. I felt a rippliness in my head from the punches and slides. I
told them that I would never tell on them and besides my family has
a pool table in our basement. Come over and use it any time. We just
don't have some things that go with it. I'll never tell on you. Come
over any time. But my head was getting pulverized, and in reality I
was already on a cloud floating up to the sky. The voices around said,
You ain't got no pool table, Your family is poor as dirt, Don't you go
on putting on airs. My lips realized, How did you know that word:
airs? Then my head got completely mashed up. Meanwhile Beanie,
Bellerina's brother, waved to me from his car and laughed because it
was truly funny seeing the smartass skinny one with the spy notebook of no-good gossip bout everyone on this block get the daylights
whipped out of her and maybe he even saw what I wrote about a guy
like him in my notebook about how strong and handsome but feeling up ladies now what a shame and why do they have to do that
when all they have to do is ask and surely someone will say, Yes Please.

Bibi and Martha had my head in a lock, and then Crater had the
stupendous idea of putting me between the cinder blocks to see if
they could make a girl sandwich. Bellerina said, It hurts the most
when something hard is lying on top of your moist spot. The other
girls looked at her funny. *Where the heck is that?* Bellerina turned her
head away. She said into the wind, Why am I the only one who ever
knows anything.

It did not get that far. They slabbed me on a cinder block and I
felt the blood bath behind my braided head go into my braided eyes
and the true way Beanie's snout nose looked came clear in my mind.
Spread out like a father's but he was only a guy. Even with that snout

nose I saw through to Beanie's handsomeness. Didn't I say so in my notebook? Next to the made up stories about Debbie Donna and Shenay there was this gorgeous guy named B. who went to prison but who was really too handsome to really do anything prisonable. He was in secret a millionaire and he was going to fix a deserving girl up in private school where they learn. Only in real life now his car says Dodge. He is handsomely driving a Dodge. Away. I felt like laughing and then the blood trinkled to the line that was my mouth, all the way into my neck, later my eyelids. The blood burned deeper the spot of lonely that was already there. We have a pool table. Only problem is we don't have the balls that go with it. Where is every Body running? Why are you going? Wait. But it was too late. I was there half a sandwich for a pillow and no way in hell Beanie in his Dodge was going to give me another look now.

At the bus stop I am always shrinking of the girls. Fall Spring Morning Bedtime Schoolclothes PJs. I want to be with them but I am also shrinking. I wish I was dumber. I wish I was getting left back. I wish I weighed a hundred twenty pounds in the fifth grade. Then I would be in the bus stop circle. I could stop feeling Bethi breathe down my plaid dress in her waiting. She stands so close. I need to do something to her, even though she will never tell on me, and that fact makes it more stupider to do it in the first place.

My mother thinks that I am incomprehensible for wishing these kinds of things. To be left back and big. My father just laughs in the background, while he is watching *60 Minutes*. He laughs, Just one look at Glory's math grades and you can tell she's gonna be in the fifth grade a long time, maybe years. I would of got a horse whipping. You don't know how easy things are nowadays. It's the state of cultural illiteracy. Then he goes back to watching. Mother adds, And another thing: You better stop bringing up private school, girl. It's just incomprehensible. Do you think we made out of money? Then Father adds, And you better stop writing in that damn notebook and write something for Mr. di Salvo that will get you passed into sixth grade. Bethi smiles at me but I don't want it. Then they go on. Mother is folding clothes and telling Bethi what to put down on her spelling worksheet and my father is saying to the tv I Been Told You That Last Year Stupid Ass and I am doing nothing important, just standing there in an invisible cloud of butterflies, roaches, and wasps, all asking me to be their best friend.

Bellerina looks me up and down in the hallway. —What you doing here?

Before I can open my mouth she says: You want me to permanently damage that shit-ass face of yours?

—Bellerina, let's you and me go to the Back. No one will know.

—Now what in Shit's Heaven do I want to go to the Back with you for? You ain't no Body. Forget it. I'ma kill you.

—Aww no, Bellerina, I have something really big to tell you out there. If you know this you will be Boss of the Girls. You will have the Power.

—What in Shit's Heaven?

—Please come with me. Then you can whip my ass in front of the whole school. Let's run to the Back. Okay? Let's run. Let's run.

Debbie ran across little Tiffany Hammond. Tiffany was in tears, and her brown curls glittered in the sun. "What is the matter, dear child?" Debbie asked. Tiffany said it was all these words she couldn't get on her spelling quiz. She was going to fail third grade. She couldn't even make up a spelling story. She sat on the steps of her apartment and wept perfoundly. Debbie put her arms around Tiffany.

"Let me help you," she said. By magic, Donna came with Shenay. The two of them explained spelling tips to little Tiffany. They taught her how to practice to win. Meanwhile Debbie thought of a story that could put together the words Gather Garnish Gaze Gazebo Generous Generosity Genuine Ghost Gibberish. They read Tiffany's story out loud and they laughed in harmony. Tiffany said, "You saved me from impending doom, all you are geniuses" and they laughed when they realized that Genius was a spelling word too.

Shenay said why don't we start a spelling club at school cause she said girls need to know more spelling words than boys so that they wouldn't be sitting on no steps in the middle of the day crying their goddamn eyes out. "Girls can be strong, Tiffany. Tears ain't always the answer." Shenay said. Donna said that a spelling club would be just fine. Donna said that she had something to discuss with Debbie in private, so goodbye Shenay. Shenay thought a minute to herself. Then she said, "Yeah, Goodbye Girls."

Bellerina and I snuck out the window over the emergency door. I sent Bethi back to her class only I didn't know if she could make it without blabbing. Me and Bellerina walked half the way to the Back. We didn't say a word. We looked over by the handball court and saw the High Schoolers smoking there. They cursed all the time but it didn't sound like the way elementary cursed. It came over elementary lips like bowling balls except Bellerina who it was her natural way of life. High Schoolers could curse up a storm and when it was over, you realized that all they said was hi how you doing? Bellerina waved to her sister standing out there with Big Susie but they didn't notice her. Gimlet had her warm arm around Big Susie's shoulder, and their faces was really next to each other. I felt my secret long heart.

Charlie came out the shack that stood in the corner of the Back. We could see him from half way. Charlie wiped his mouth along the edges with his pointer finger and his thumb. He was big and small at the same time. He waved to us to come. "I'm feeling warm!" he shouted. He was leaning against the shack.

Bellerina looked a bit scared. She turned to me. —So what you want? What you got to tell me?

I swallowed. —Bellerina. I don't want to fight anymore. What is it about me you don't like? I can change! My notebook is only stories. Of how things can maybe be. I am really smarter than people think. I can change! Bellerina!

—I don't like your fucking face. Can you change that?

I also don't like your slobbering re-tard sister. Why she have to stand with us?

I also don't like it you think you are better than me. You think you a Brainiac. Well let me tell you. That's a damn lie. Write that in your damn notebook full of lies. Four Eye Fuck In Liar. You hurt a lot of people with them damn lies. That's what you are.

Bellerina walked away just like that. So my plan had failed. I just kept my head down and my eyes closed. Bellerina walked to the shack. It was a stupid plan when you got right down to it.

I sighed with the future. Your Body never gets used to it. It hurts more each time. I de-test the feeling of hands messing me up. I am a girl made out of brown peel, not iron and steel. I also de-test the eyes. They can mess you in a way that makes you afraid to sleep at night, get up in the morning. The eyes can push you off into a lonely circle, like the circle of me and my sister, like the circle of me. I de-test it all.

Bellerina called back to me —I'ma get you this afternoon. Me and the girls. You better be ready. Drag me out in the cold. You lucky Charlie is here for me.

She went with Charlie in the shack. Charlie said "Dag! Dag!" and I saw other High Schoolers fastwalking there. She had said: I'm his whole world.

Bellerina's sister Gimlet shook her head when she saw Bellerina going in the shack. Big Susie grinned. Gimlet usually doesn't care, even when she swears she will kick anyone's butt who messes with her little sister. She took a puff of cigarillo, down to her feet. She looked and shaked her head. Big Susie laughed, "She's going to get *lit up.*"

They were needed again. Little Bobby Lee had fallen off his sister's ba-nana seat bike and was bleeding. Another boy stood near him. "Help!" the big boy cried. Soon a crowd was there. No one was capable of doing nothing. Lucky for them Debbie, Donna and Shenay was speeding on their way to the place.

"What happened?" Debbie asked. The big boy told her. The crowd agreed. Bobby was so clumsy when you weren't looking. His sister was in tears.

Shenay stepped up and looked at the big boy. She waited a moment with eyes that didn't move. She said, "I'm waiting." The crowd growed silent. The sun didn't move from the sky. She said, "I'll wait." The big boy looked. A river of pee ran down his leg and he bawled. "It was not all my fault," he bawled.

Shenay stepped back. The crowd laughed and started smacking the big boy upside his head. Someone held little Bobby Lee in their arms and rocked him to sleep like a scared hummingbird. Shenay stepped back until she was just a speck on the distance.

I sat down on the steps of the handball court, and out the stretch of my eye, I could see the shack at the Back. High Schoolers went in and they stayed. The sky hung blue. Gimlet walked over to me out of nowhere. I had to catch my breathing. I was thinking about burning my notebook. It was just a bunch of stories. A fire would prove something. Or I could take cinder blocks and make a sandwich. That would be better proof.

Gimlet stopped in front of me and said she heard I was going to get my ass kicked. That's what she heard. She looked over at the shack. She shrugged her shoulders. But then she just kept on walking, like the air was not holding her down.

Shenay called a special meeting. It was at her family's ski lodge, and her parents were both away on a medical mission in the Heart of Africa. "I want to speak to you both from my soul," she explained to the girls.

She pulled Darnell Williams out her closet. "Is this the boy you two been dreaming about?" The girls nodded yes. "Well, stop it right now. We have a large mission at hand. What will happen if we don't save things?" The two others didn't have anything to say in their shame. "What will happen if we ain't responsible for the lips and knees and heads and hearts of others?"

Shenay took Darnell Williams and kissed his mouth into her own. She put his face on her chest and said, "There. Ooh there." She told him, "Also: Kissing me on my neck drives me wild. Now you going to have to give me what you been giving these two." There was no arguing with Shenay.

The other two said, "We understand" and went on home to do their social studies homework. They realized that Shenay could have it all, but she was doing this to be responsible. She taught them a uplifting lesson about girls in the life of the world.

In the corner of my eye I saw Bellerina fastwalk out the shack in the Back. She was saying something but then Charlie pulled her back in. Her shirt was open. I could see the sides of it blowing in the wind. I could see that she was not wearing a undershirt but a womanly brassiere.

In the hallway Gimlet was talking to Principal Blackburn. Big Susie was nodding yes to everything. Gimlet cried, And if my god-damn sister can't be learning here in school I'ma go to the damn super-in-ten-den to get some answers. You suppose to be watching over these kids. And they hanging all over the place who knows where doing shit.

Principal Blackburn said, Gimlet it's good that you watch out for Bellerina. She's been having trouble. Why hasn't your mother called? Or your father? We need your parents to take action.

—I'm her parent. Shit. I'm just as good.

—This is really the job of a father, Gimlet. You are pretty young yourself. Please send your father in to see me.

—You see Big Susie? Well, she is Bellerina's father, if I say so. Get that through your thick head, Mrs. Blackburn. Shit.

Shenay pushed Darnell Williams out a five story window. His Body was a blood bath. She didn't have time for that kind of mess. She knew there was more important things in life besides girls loving boys. Why do girls always be helping others? Why don't girls grow up to be mad scientists? Why don't girls grow up and love other girls and fight over them instead of boys? The world had too many fences in it for Shenay. She called the ambulance to come and pick up the blood bath.

Mr. di Salvo came outside and grabbed my shoulder. Bethi was next to him, looking guilty in her slow way. She knew I was going to fix her. Mr. di Salvo asked, "What the hell are you doing out here?" pulling me back into Park Avenue. He dragged me past Gimlet and Mrs. Blackburn. Mr. di Salvo listened and took out his hanky and wiped the sweat off his lip. "Hell," he said.

He turned to me. "You are lucky your sister blabbed. You trying to get your butt beat? Always looking for a way out of math. You barely passed the test from last Wednesday. But just how would you know that, Glory? You just sitting out here enjoying the day when the rest of us are looking over the math answers. You. You. You. You. You."

I looked at my sister before we dumped her off at Mr. Flegenheimer's. I could not think of any big evil to scare her with. She blinked at me. I growled, What you want, Bethi? Stop wasting my precious time. Stop looking at me. Wipe your nose. Close your damn mouth.

But Bethi put her nose close to my shoulder. She sniffed me. She whispered so only I could hear, I don't want you get beat up Glory. I going to help you. We going to poison them. We going to kill them so we can stand back together. I want to be with you. We going to make poison.

I stopped. I hugged my sister. I didn't care. I hugged her till we got to Mr. Flegenheimer's, where the kids were screaming like gorillas from behind the door. Mr. di Salvo made me let her go.

Shenay didn't let her mind go down, like some other girls she knew. She concentrated. When she saw a girl, she did not try to explain it that the wind or the stars or the pencils told her to do it. She did not have to go crazy in her head to feel the genuine things. She walked up to the girl and held her in her arms and said, "You are my present to me." That's all there was to it. She would always help Those In Need, Shenay would. She did not have to be a nutcase.

Big Susie saw me and walked next to me on the way back to Mr. di Salvo's class. Mr. di Salvo held my arm tight. He was thinking about how I had been a different girl. That meant *zero* girls punishment. But by the time we got to our classroom, Mr. di Salvo was thinking of letting me be in the chorus to sing one of the assembly songs. He said I would have to learn the words and not just goof off with my head in the clouds like I am prone to do. Could I learn the words and not be a screwball. Mr. di Salvo was feeling for me and that was a good surprise.

Big Susie was walking next to me. She leaned over and her chest touched me on the shoulder. She whispered in my ear that I was not getting beat up that day or on any day. Bellerina was not going to get me. Bellerina was not going to get anyone. Big Susie touched my hair with her hand. She said, You girls are scared shitless. Then you go and do some shit. Just wait. And then Big Susie was gone.

I'se going back to Dixie
No More I'se gwine back to wander,
My Heart's Turned Back to Dixie
I can't stay here no longer
I miss de old plantation, my friends and my relation,
My heart's turned back to Dixie, and I must go.

I've hoed in fields of cotton
I've worked up on de river
I used to think if I got off
I'd go back there, no never
But time has changed de ole man, His head is bending low
His heart's turned back to Dixie, and I must go.

I sat in the desk in the back of the room, next to Martha Madison. She tried to look rough and scare me into last year, but I kept my eyes right on her till she looked away. The venetian blinds asked me how I felt. The pencil groove in my desk wanted to know why I wasn't talking to it anymore. I said out loud, I don't want you. *No more.* Martha Madison winked her eyes in the other direction trying to do like I was crazy. Only I wasn't.

You can change things just by ignoring the furniture. You can get your own kind of strength. I looked hard at Martha Madison. From the side, her eyelids had on a trace of her mother's eye makeup, Blue Oceans. Martha always stold her mother's makeup to come to school in. She had dreams. The desk wood was silent. The venetian blinds were just venetian blinds. I looked hard at Martha. I also had dreams. I will keep my notebook in my schoolbag. That's the proof. I will get back in that circle.

BICH MINH NGUYEN

The Good Immigrant Student

My stepmother, Rosa, who began dating my father when I was three years old, says that my sister and I used to watch *Police Woman* and rapturously repeat everything Angie Dickinson said. But when the show was over Anh and I would resume our Vietnamese, whispering together, giggling in accents. Rosa worried about this. She had the idea that she could teach us English and we could teach her Vietnamese. She would make us lunch or give us baths, speaking slowly and asking us how to say *water,* or *rice,* or *house.*

After she and my father married, Rosa swept us out of our falling-down house and into middle-class suburban Grand Rapids, Michigan. Our neighborhood surrounded Ken-O-Sha Elementary School and Plaster Creek, and was only a short drive away from the original Meijer's Thrifty Acres. In the early 1980s, this neighborhood of mismatching street names—Poinsettia, Van Auken, Senora, Ravanna—was home to families of Dutch heritage, and everyone was Christian Reformed, and conservative Republican. Except us. Even if my father hadn't left his rusted-through silver Mustang, the first car he ever owned, to languish in the driveway for months we would have stuck out simply because we weren't white. There was my Latina stepmother and her daughter, Cristina, my father, sister, grandmother, and I, refugees from Saigon; and my half-brother born a year after we moved to the house on Ravanna Street.

Although my family lived two blocks from Ken-O-Sha, my step-mother enrolled me and Anh at Sherwood Elementary, a bus ride away, because Sherwood had a bilingual education program. Rosa, who had a master's in education and taught ESL and community ed in the public school system, was a big supporter of bilingual education. School mornings, Anh and I would be at the bus stop at the corner of our street quite early, hustled out of the house by our grandmother who constantly feared we would miss our chance. I went off to first grade, Anh to second. At ten o'clock, we crept out of our classes, drawing glances and whispers from the other students, and convened with a group of Vietnamese kids from other grades to learn English. The teachers were Mr. Ho, who wore a lot of short-sleeved button-down shirts in neutral hues, and Miss Huong, who favored a maroon blouse with puffy shoulders and slight ruffles at the high neck and wrists, paired with a tweed skirt that hung heavily to her ankles. They passed out photocopied booklets of Vietnamese phrases and their English translations, with themes such as "In the Grocery Store." They asked us to repeat slowly after them and took turns coming around to each of us, bending close to hear our pronunciations.

Anh and I exchanged a lot of worried glances, for we had a secret that we were quite embarrassed about: we already knew English. It was the Vietnamese part that gave us trouble. When Mr. Ho and Miss Huong gave instructions, or passed out homework assignments, they did so in Vietnamese. Anh and I received praise for our English, but were reprimanded for failing to complete our assignments and failing to pay attention. After a couple of weeks of this Anh announced to Rosa that we didn't need bilingual education. Nonsense, she said. Our father just shrugged his shoulders. After that, Anh began skipping bilingual classes, urging me to do the same, and then we never went back. What was amazing was that no one, not Mrs. Eunice, my first grade teacher, or Mrs. Hankins, Anh's teacher, or even Mr. Ho or Miss Huong said anything directly to us about it. Or if they did, I have forgotten it entirely. Then one day my parents got a call from Miss Huong. When Rosa came to talk to me and Anh about it we were watching television the way kids do, sitting alarmingly close to the screen. Rosa confronted us with "Do you girls know English?" Then she suddenly said, "Do you know Vietnamese?" I can't remember what we replied to either question.

For many years, a towering old billboard over the expressway downtown proudly declared Grand Rapids "An All-American City." For me, that all-American designation meant all-white. I couldn't believe (and still don't) that they meant to include the growing Mexican-American population, or the sudden influx of Vietnamese refugees in 1975. I often thought it a rather mean-spirited prank of some administrator at the INS, deciding with a flourish of a signature to send a thousand refugees to Grand Rapids, a city that boasted having more churches per square mile than other city in the United States. Did that administrator know what Grand Rapids was like? That in school, everywhere I turned, and often when I closed my eyes, I saw blond blond blond? The point of bilingual education was assimilation. To my stepmother, the point was preservation: she didn't want English to take over wholly, pushing the Vietnamese out of our heads. She was too ambitious. Anh and I were Americanized as soon as we turned on the television. Today, bilingual education is supposed to have become both a method of assimilation and a method of preservation, an effort to prove that kids can have it both ways. They can supposedly keep English for school and their friends and keep another language for home and family.

In Grand Rapids, Michigan, in the 1980s, I found that an impossible task.

I transferred to Ken-O-Sha Elementary in time for third grade, after Rosa finally admitted that taking the bus all the way to Sherwood was pointless. I was glad to transfer, eager to be part of a class that wasn't, in my mind, tainted with the knowledge of my bilingual stigma. Third grade was led by Mrs. Alexander, an imperious, middle-aged woman of many plaid skirts held safe by giant gold safety pins. She had a habit of turning her wedding ring around and around her finger while she stood at the chalkboard. Mrs. Alexander had an intricate system of rewards for good grades and good behavior, denoted by colored star stickers on a piece of poster board that loomed over us all. One glance and you could see who was behind, who was striding ahead.

I was an insufferably good student, with perfect Palmer cursive and the highest possible scores in every subject. I had learned this trick at Sherwood. That the quieter you are, the shyer and sweeter and better-at-school you are, the more the teacher will let you alone. Mrs. Alexander should have let me alone. For, in addition to my excellent marks, I was nearly silent, deadly shy, and wholly obedient. My greatest fear was being called on, or in any way standing out more than I already did in the class that was, except for me and one black student, dough-white. I got good grades because I feared the authority of the teacher; I felt that getting in good with Mrs. Alexander would protect me, that she would protect me from the frightful rest of the world. But Mrs. Alexander was not agreeable to this notion. If it was my turn to read aloud during reading circle, she'd interrupt me to snap, "You're reading too fast" or demand, "What does that word mean?" Things she did not do to the other students. Anh, when I told her about this, suggested that perhaps Mrs. Alexander liked me and wanted to help me get smarter. But neither of us believed it. You know when a teacher likes you and when she doesn't.

Secretly, I admired and envied the rebellious kids, like Robbie Andrews who came to school looking bleary-eyed and pinched, like a hungover adult; Robbie and his ilk snapped back at teachers, were routinely sent to the principal's office, were even spanked a few times with the principal's infamous red paddle (apparently no one in Grand Rapids objected to corporal punishment). Those kids made noise, possessed something I thought was confidence, self-knowledge, allowing them to marvelously question everything ordered of them. They had the ability to challenge the given world.

Toward the middle of third grade Mrs. Alexander introduced a stuffed lion to the pool of rewards: the best student of the week would earn the privilege of having the lion sit on his or her desk for the entire week. My quantity of gold stars was neck and neck with that of my two competitors, Brenda and Jennifer, both sweet-eyed blond girls with pastel-colored monogrammed sweaters and neatly tied Dock-Sides. My family did not have a lot of money and my step-mother had terrible taste. Thus I attended school in such ensembles as dark red parachute pants and a nubby pink sweater stitched with a picture of a unicorn rearing up. This only propelled me to try harder to be good, to make up for everything I felt was against me: my odd family, my race, my very face. And I craved that stuffed lion. Week after week, the lion perched on Brenda's desk or Jennifer's desk. Meanwhile, the class spelling bee approached. I didn't know I was such a good speller until I won it, earning a scalloped-edged certificate and a candy bar. That afternoon I started toward home, then remembered I'd forgotten my rain boots in my locker. I doubled back to school and overheard Mrs. Alexander in the classroom talking to another teacher. "Can you believe it?" Mrs. Alexander was saying. "A foreigner winning our spelling bee!"

I waited for the stuffed lion the rest of that year, with a kind of patience I have no patience for today. To no avail. In June, on the last day of school, Mrs. Alexander gave the stuffed lion to Brenda to keep forever.

The first time I had to read aloud something I had written—perhaps it was in fourth grade—I felt such terror, such a need not to have any attention upon me, that I convinced myself that I had become invisible, that the teacher could never call on me because she couldn't see me.

More than once, I was given the assignment of writing a report about my family history. I loathed this task, for I was dreadfully aware that my history could not be faked; it already showed on my face. When my turn came to read out loud the teacher had to ask me several times to speak louder. Some kids, a few of them older, in different classes, took to pressing back the corners of their eyes with the heels of their palms while they chanted, "Ching-chong, ching-chong!" during recess. (This continued until Anh, who was far tougher than me, threatened to beat them up.)

I have no way of telling what tortured me more: the actual snickers and remarks and watchfulness of my classmates, or my own imagination, conjuring disdain. My own sense of shame. At times I felt sickened by my obedience, my accumulation of gold stickers, my every effort to be invisible.

Yet Robbie Andrews must have felt the same kind of claustrophobia, trapped in his own reputation, in his ability to be otherwise. I learned in school that changing oneself is not easy, that the world makes up its mind quickly.

I've heard that Robbie dropped out of high school, got a girl pregnant, found himself in and out of first juvenile detention, then jail.

What comes out of difference? What constitutes difference? Such questions, academic and unanswered, popped up in every other course description in college. But the idea of difference is easy to come by, especially in school; it is shame, the permutations and inversions of difference and self-loathing, that we should be worrying about.

Imagined torment, imagined scorn. When what is imagined and what is desired turn on each other.

Some kids want to rebel; other kids want to disappear. I wanted to disappear. I was not brave enough to shrug my shoulders and flaunt my difference; because I could not disappear into the crowd, I wished to disappear entirely. Anyone might have mistaken this for passivity.

Once, at the end of my career at Sherwood Elementary, I disappeared on the bus home. Mine was usually the third stop, but that day the bus driver thought I wasn't there, and she sailed right by the corner of Ravanna and Senora. I said nothing. The bus wove its way downtown, and for the first time I got to see where other children lived, some of them in clean orderly neighborhoods, some near houses with sagging porches and boarded-up windows. All the while, the kid sitting across the aisle from me played the same cheerful song over and over on his portable boom box. *Pass the doochee from the left hand side, pass the doochee from the left hand side.* He and his brother turned out to be the last kids off the bus. Then the bus driver saw me through the rearview mirror. She walked back to where I was sitting and said, "How come you didn't get off at your stop?" I shook my head, don't know. She sighed and drove me home.

I was often doing that, shaking my head silently or staring up wordlessly. I realize that while I remember so much of what other people said when I was a child, I remember little of what I said. Probably because I didn't say much at all.

I recently came across in the stacks of the University of Michigan library *A Manual for Indochinese Refugee Education 1976–1977*. Some of it is silly, but much of it is a painstaking, fairly thoughtful effort to let school administrators and teachers know how to go about sensitively handling the influx of Vietnamese children in the public schools. Here is one of the most wonderful items of advice: "The Vietnamese child, even the older child, is also reported to be afraid of the dark, and more often than not, believes in ghosts. A teacher may have to be a little more solicitous of the child on gloomy, wintery days." Perhaps if Mrs. Alexander had read this, she would not have upbraided me so often for tracking mud into the classroom on rainy days. In third grade I was horrified and ashamed of my muddy shoes. I hung back, trying to duck behind this or that dark-haired boy. In spite of this, in spite of bilingual education, and shyness, and all that wordless shaking of my head, I was sent off every Monday to the Spectrum School for the Gifted and Talented. I still have no idea who selected me, who singled me out. Spectrum was (and still is) a public school program that invited students from every public elementary school to meet once a week and take specialized classes on topics such as the Middle Ages, Ellis Island, and fairy tales. Each student chose two classes, a major and minor, and for the rest of the semester worked toward final projects in both. I loved going to Spectrum. Not only did the range of students from other schools prove to be diverse, I found myself feeling more comfortable, mainly because Spectrum encouraged individual work. And the teachers seemed happy to be there. The best teacher at Spectrum was Mrs. King, whom every student adored. I still remember the soft gray sweaters she wore, her big wavy hair, her art-class handwriting, the way she'd often tell us to close our eyes when she read us a particular story or passage.

I believe that I figured out how to stop disappearing, how to talk and answer, even speak up, after several years in Spectrum. I was still deeply self-conscious, but I became able, sometimes, to maneuver around it.

Spectrum may have spoiled me a little, because it made me think about college and freedom, and thus made all the years in between disappointing and annoying.

In seventh grade I joined Anh and Cristina at the City School, a seventh through twelfth grade public school in the Grand Rapids system that served as an early charter school; admission was by interview, and each grade had about fifty students. The City School had the advantage of being downtown, perched over old cobblestone roads, and close to the main public library. Art and music history were required. There were no sports teams. And volunteering was mandatory. But kids didn't tend to stay at City School; as they got older they transferred to one of the big high schools nearby, perhaps wishing to play sports, perhaps wishing to get away from City's rather brutal academic system. Each half semester, after grades were doled out, giant dot-matrix printouts of everyone's GPAs were posted in the hallways.

I didn't stay at City, either. When my family moved to a different suburb, my stepmother promptly transferred me to Forest Hills Northern High School. Most of the students there came from upper-middle-class or very well-to-do families; the ones who didn't stood out sharply. The rich kids were the same as they were anywhere in America: they wore a lot of Esprit and Guess, drove nice cars, and ran student council, prom, and sports. These kids strutted down the hallways; the boys sat in a row on the long windowsill near a group of lockers, whistling or calling out to girls who walked by. Girls gathered in bathrooms with their Clinique lipsticks.

High school was the least interesting part of my education, but I did accomplish something: I learned to forget myself a little. I learned the sweetness of apathy. And through apathy, how to forget my skin and body for a minute or two, almost not caring what would happen if I walked into a room late and all heads swiveled toward me. I learned the pleasure that reveals itself in the loss, no matter how slight, of self-consciousness. These things occurred because I remained the good immigrant student, without raising my hand often or showing off what I knew. Doing work was rote, and I went along to get along. I've never gotten over the terror of being called on in class, or the dread in knowing that I'm expected to contribute to class discussion. But there is a slippage between being good and being unnoticed, and in that sliver of freedom I learned what it could feel like to walk in the world in plain, unself-conscious view.

I would like to make a broad, accurate statement about immigrant children in schools. I would like to speak for them (us). I hesitate; I cannot. My own sister, for instance, was never as shy as I was. Anh disliked school from the start, choosing rebellion rather than silence. It was a good arrangement: I wrote papers for her and she paid me in money or candy; she gave me rides to school if I promised not to tell anyone about her cigarettes. Still, I think of an Indian friend of mine who told of an elementary school experience in which a blond schoolchild told the teacher, "I can't sit by her. My mom said I can't sit by anyone who's brown." And another friend, whose family immigrated around the same time mine did, whose second grade teacher used her as a vocabulary example: "Children, this is what a *foreigner* is." And sometimes I fall into thinking that kids today have the advantage of so much more wisdom, that they are so much more socially and politically aware than anyone was when I was in school. But I am wrong, of course. I know not every kid is fortunate enough to have a teacher like Mrs. King, or a program like Spectrum, or even the benefit of a manual written by a group of concerned educators; I know that some kids want to disappear and disappear until they actually do. Sometimes I think I see them, in the blurry background of a magazine photo, or in a gaggle of kids following a teacher's aide across the street. The kids with heads bent down, holding themselves in such a way that they seem to be self-conscious even of how they breathe. Small, shy, quiet kids, such good, good kids, *immigrant, foreigner,* their eyes watchful and waiting for whatever judgment will occur. I reassure myself that they will grow up fine, they will be okay. Maybe I cross the same street, then another, glancing back once in a while to see where they are going.

DAVID SEDARIS

I Like Guys

Shortly before I graduated from eighth grade, it was announced that, come fall, our county school system would adopt a policy of racial integration by way of forced busing. My Spanish teacher broke the news in a way she hoped might lead us to a greater understanding of her beauty and generosity.

"I remember the time I was at the state fair, standing in line for a Sno-Kone," she said, fingering the kiss curls that framed her squat, compact face. "And a little colored girl ran up and tugged at my skirt, asking if she could touch my hair. 'Just once,' she said. 'Just one time for good luck.'

"Now, I don't know about the rest of you, but my hair means a lot to me." The members of my class nodded to signify that their hair meant a lot to them as well. They inched forward in their seats, eager to know where this story might be going. Perhaps the little Negro girl was holding a concealed razor blade. Maybe she was one of the troublemakers out for a fresh white scalp.

I sat marveling at their naïveté. Like all her previous anecdotes, this woman's story was headed straight up her ass.

"I checked to make sure she didn't have any candy on her hands, and then I bent down and let this little colored girl touch my hair." The teacher's eyes assumed the dewy, faraway look she reserved for such Hallmark moments. "Then this little fudge-colored girl put her

hand on my cheek and said, 'Oh,' she said, 'I wish I could be white
and pretty like you.'" She paused, positioning herself on the edge of
the desk as though she were posing for a portrait the federal government might use on a stamp commemorating gallantry. "The thing
to remember," she said, "is that more than anything in this world,
those colored people wish they were white."

I wasn't buying it. This was the same teacher who when announcing her pregnancy said, "I just pray that my firstborn is a boy. I'll have
a boy and then maybe later I'll have a girl, because when you do it
the other way round, there's a good chance the boy will turn out to
be funny."

"'Funny,' as in having no arms and legs?" I asked.

"That," the teacher said, "is far from funny. That is tragic, and
you, sir, should have your lips sewn shut for saying such a cruel and
ugly thing. When I say 'funny,' I mean funny as in . . ." She relaxed
her wrist, allowing her hand to dangle and flop. "I mean 'funny' as
in *that* kind of funny." She minced across the room, but it failed to
illustrate her point, as this was more or less her natural walk, a series
of gamboling little steps, her back held straight, giving the impression she was balancing something of value atop her empty head. My
seventh-period math teacher did a much better version. Snatching a
purse off the back of a student's chair, he would prance about the
room, batting his eyes and blowing kisses at the boys seated in the
front row. "So fairy nice to meet you," he'd say.

Fearful of drawing any attention to myself, I hooted and
squawked along with the rest of the class, all the while thinking,
That's me he's talking about. If I was going to make fun of people, I
had to expect a little something in return, that seemed only fair. Still,
though, it bothered me that they'd found such an easy way to get a
laugh. As entertainers, these teachers were nothing, zero. They could
barely impersonate themselves. "Look at you!" my second-period
gym teacher would shout, his sneakers squealing against the basketball court. "You're a group of ladies, a pack of tap-dancing queers."

The other boys shrugged their shoulders or smiled down at their
shoes. They reacted as if they had been called Buddhists or vampires;
sure, it was an insult, but no one would ever mistake them for the real

thing. Had they ever chanted in the privacy of their backyard temple or slept in a coffin, they would have felt the sting of recognition and shared my fear of discovery.

I had never done anything with another guy and literally prayed that I never would. As much as I fantasized about it, I understood that there could be nothing worse than making it official. You'd seen them on television from time to time, the homosexuals, maybe on one of the afternoon talk shows. No one ever came out and called them a queer, but you could just tell by their voices as they flattered the host and proclaimed great respect for their fellow guests. These were the celebrities never asked about their home life, the comedians running scarves beneath their toupees or framing their puffy faces with their open palms in an effort to eliminate the circles beneath their eyes. "The poor man's face lift," my mother called it. Regardless of their natty attire, these men appeared sweaty and desperate, willing to play the fool in exchange for the studio applause they seemed to mistake for love and acceptance. I saw something of myself in their mock weary delivery, in the way they crossed their legs and laughed at their own jokes. I pictured their homes: the finicky placement of their throw rugs and sectional sofas, the magazines carefully fanned just so upon the coffee tables with no wives or children to disturb their order. I imagined the pornography hidden in their closets and envisioned them powerless and sobbing as the police led them away in shackles, past the teenage boy who stood bathed in the light of the television news camera and shouted, "That's him! He's the one who touched my hair!"

It was my hope to win a contest, cash in the prizes, and use the money to visit a psychiatrist who might cure me of having homosexual thoughts. Electroshock, brain surgery, hypnotism—I was willing to try anything. Under a doctor's supervision, I would buckle down and really change, I swore I would.

My parents knew a couple whose son had killed a Presbyterian minister while driving drunk. They had friends whose eldest daughter had sprinkled a Bundt cake with Comet, and knew of a child who, high on spray paint, had set fire to the family's cocker spaniel. Yet, they spoke of no one whose son was a homosexual. The odds struck me as bizarre, but the message was the same: this was clearly the worst thing that could happen to a person. The day-to-day anxiety was bad enough without my instructors taking their feeble little potshots. If my math teacher were able to subtract the alcohol from his diet, he'd still be on the football field where he belonged; and my Spanish teacher's credentials were based on nothing more than a long weekend in Tijuana, as far as I could tell. I quit taking their tests and completing their homework assignments, accepting Fs rather than delivering the grades I thought might promote their reputations as good teachers. It was a strategy that hurt only me, but I thought it cunning. We each had our self-defeating schemes, all the boys I had come to identify as homosexuals. Except for a few transfer students, I had known most of them since the third grade. We'd spent years gathered together in cinder-block offices as one speech therapist after another tried to cure us of our lisps. Had there been a walking specialist, we probably would have met there, too. These were the same boys who carried poorly forged notes to gym class and were the first to raise their hands when the English teacher asked for a volunteer to read aloud from *The Yearling* or *Lord of the Flies*. We had long ago identified one another and understood that because of everything we had in common, we could never be friends. To socialize would have drawn too much attention to ourselves. We were members of a secret society founded on self-loathing. When a teacher or classmate made fun of a real homosexual, I made certain my laugh was louder than anyone else's. When a club member's clothing was thrown into the locker-room toilet, I was always the first to cheer. When it was my clothing, I watched as the faces of my fellows broke into recognizable expressions of relief. *Faggots,* I thought. *This should have been you.*

Several of my teachers, when discussing the upcoming school integration, would scratch at the damp stains beneath their arms, pulling back their lips to reveal every bit of tooth and gum. They made monkey noises, a manic succession of ohhs and ahhs meant to suggest that soon our school would be no different than a jungle. Had a genuine ape been seated in the room, I guessed he might have identified their calls as a cry of panic. Anything that caused them suffering brought me joy, but I doubted they would talk this way come fall.

From everything I'd seen on television, the Negros would never stand for such foolishness. As a people, they seemed to stick together. They knew how to fight, and I hoped that once they arrived, the battle might come down to the gladiators, leaving the rest of us alone.

At the end of the school year, my sister Lisa and I were excused from our volunteer jobs and sent to Greece to attend a month-long summer camp advertised as "the Crown Jewel of the Ionian Sea." The camp was reserved exclusively for Greek Americans and featured instruction in such topics as folk singing and something called "religious prayer and flag." I despised the idea of summer camp but longed to boast that I had been to Europe. "It changes people!" our neighbor had said. Following a visit to Saint-Tropez, she had marked her garden with a series of tissue-sized international flags. A once discreet and modest woman, she now paraded about her yard wearing nothing but clogs and a flame-stitched bikini. "Europe is the best thing that can happen to a person, especially if you like wine!"

I saw Europe as an opportunity to re-invent myself. I might still look and speak the same way, but having walked those cobblestoned streets, I would be identified as Continental. "He has a passport," my classmates would whisper. "Quick, let's run before he judges us!"

I told myself that I would find a girlfriend in Greece. She would be a French tourist wandering the beach with a loaf of bread beneath her arm. Lisette would prove that I wasn't a homosexual, but a man with refined tastes. I saw us holding hands against the silhouette of the Acropolis, the girl begging me to take her accordion as a memento of our love. "Silly you," I would say, brushing the tears from her eyes, "just give me the beret, that will be enough to hold you in my heart until the end of time."

In case no one believed me, I would have my sister as a witness. Lisa and I weren't getting along very well, but I hoped that the warm Mediterranean waters might melt the icicle she seemed to have mistaken for a rectal thermometer. Faced with a country of strangers, she would have no choice but to appreciate my company.

Our father accompanied us to New York, where we met our fellow campers for the charter flight to Athens. There were hundreds of them, each one confident and celebratory. They tossed their complimentary Aegean Airlines tote bags across the room, shouting and jostling one another. This would be the way I'd act once we'd finally returned from camp, but not one moment before. Were it an all-girl's camp, I would have been able to work up some enthusiasm. Had they sent me alone to pry leeches off the backs of blood-thirsty Pygmies, I might have gone bravely—but spending a month in a dormitory full of boys, that was asking too much. I'd tried to put it out of my mind, but faced with their boisterous presence, I found myself growing progressively more hysterical. My nervous tics shifted into their highest gear, and a small crowd gathered to watch what they believed to be an exotic folk dance. If my sister was anxious about our trip, she certainly didn't show it. Prying my fingers off her wrist, she crossed the room and introduced herself to a girl who stood picking salvageable butts out of the standing ashtray. This was a tough-looking Queens native named Stefani Heartattackus or Testicock-ules. I recall only that her last name had granted her a lifelong supply of resentment. Stefani wore mirrored aviator sunglasses and carried an oversized comb in the back pocket of her hiphugger jeans. Of all the girls in the room, she seemed the least likely candidate for my sis-ter's friendship. They sat beside each other on the plane, and by the time we disembarked in Athens, Lisa was speaking in a very bad Queens accent. During the long flight, while I sat cowering beside a boy named Seamen, my sister had undergone a complete physical and cultural transformation. Her shoulder-length hair was now parted on the side, covering the left half of her face as if to conceal a nasty scar. She cursed and spat, scowling out the window of the char-tered bus as if she'd come to Greece with the sole intention of kicking its dusty ass. "What a shithole," she yelled. "Jeez, if I'd knowed it was gonna be dis hot, I woulda stayed home wit my headdin da oven, right, girls!"

It shamed me to hear my sister struggle so hard with an accent that did nothing but demean her, yet I silently congratulated her on the attempt. I approached her once we reached the camp, a cluster of whitewashed buildings hugging the desolate coast, far from any neighboring village.

"Listen, asshole," she said, "as far as this place is concerned, I don't know you and you sure as shit don't know me, you got that?" She spoke as if she were auditioning for a touring company of *West Side Story*, one hand on her hip and the other fingering her pocket comb as if it were a switchblade.

"Hey, Carolina!" one of her new friends called.

"A righta ready," she brayed. "I'm comin', I'm comin'."

That was the last time we spoke before returning home. Lisa had adjusted with remarkable ease, but something deep in my stomach suggested I wouldn't thrive nearly as well. Camp lasted a month, during which time I never once had a bowel movement. I was used to having a semiprivate bathroom and could not bring myself to occupy one of the men's room stalls, fearful that someone might recognize my shoes or, even worse, not see my shoes at all and walk in on me. Sitting down three times a day for a heavy Greek meal became an exercise akin to packing a musket. I told myself I'd sneak off during one of our field trips, but those toilets were nothing more than a hole in the floor, a hole I could have filled with no problem whatsoever. I considered using the Ionian Sea, but for some unexplained reason, we were not allowed to swim in those waters. The camp had an Olympic-size pool that was fed from the sea and soon grew murky with stray bits of jellyfish that had been pulverized by the pump. The tiny tentacles raised welts on campers' skin, so shortly after arriving, it was announced that we could photograph both the pool *and* the ocean but could swim in neither. The Greeks had invented democracy, built the Acropolis, and then called it a day. Our swimming period was converted into "contemplation hour" for the girls and an extended soccer practice for the boys.

"I really think I'd be better off contemplating," I told the coach, massaging my distended stomach. "I've got a personal problem that's sort of weighing me down."

Because we were first and foremost Americans, the camp was basically an extension of junior high school except that here everyone had an excess of moles or a single eyebrow. The attractive sports-minded boys ran the show, currying favor from the staff and ruining our weekly outdoor movie with their inane heckling. From time to time the rented tour buses would carry us to view one of the country's many splendors, and we would raid the gift shops, stealing anything that wasn't chained to the shelf or locked in a guarded case. These were cheap, plated puzzle rings and pint-size vases, little pom-pommed shoes, and coffee mugs reading SPARTA IS FOR A LOVER. My shoplifting experience was the only thing that gave me an edge over the popular boys. "Hold it like this," I'd whisper. "Then swivel around and slip the statue of Diana down the back of your shorts, covering it with your T-shirt. Remember to back out the door while leaving and never forget to wave good-bye."

There was one boy at camp I felt I might get along with, a Detroit native named Jason who slept on the bunk beneath mine. Jason tended to look away when talking to the other boys, shifting his eyes as though he were studying the weather conditions. Like me, he used his free time to curl into a fetal position, staring at the bedside calendar upon which he'd x-ed out all the days he had endured so far. We were finishing our 7:15 to 7:45 wash-and-rinse segment one morning when our dormitory counselor arrived for inspection shouting, "What are you, a bunch of goddamned faggots who can't make your beds?"

I giggled out loud at his stupidity. If anyone knew how to make a bed, it was a faggot. It was the others he needed to worry about. I saw Jason laughing, too, and soon we took to mocking this counselor, re-ferring to each other first as "faggots" and then as "stinking faggots." We were "lazy faggots" and "sunburned faggots" before we eventu-ally became "faggoty faggots." We couldn't protest the word, as that would have meant acknowledging the truth of it. The most we could do was embrace it as a joke. Embodying the term in all its clichéd glory, we minced and pranced about the room for each other's enter-tainment when the others weren't looking. I found myself easily out-performing my teachers, who had failed to capture the proper spirit of loopy bravado inherent in the role. *Faggot,* as a word, was always delivered in a harsh, unforgiving tone befitting those weak or stupid enough to act upon their impulses. We used it as a joke, an accusa-tion, and finally as a dare. Late at night I'd feel my bunk buck and sway, knowing that Jason was either masturbating or beating eggs for an omelette. *Is it me he's thinking about?* I'd follow his lead and wake the next morning to find our entire iron-frame unit had wandered a good eighteen inches away from the wall. Our love had the power to move bunks.

Having no willpower, we depended on circumstances to keep us apart. *This cannot happen* was accompanied by the sound of bedsprings whining, *Oh, but maybe just this once.* There came an afternoon when, running late for flag worship, we found ourselves alone in the dormitory. What started off as name-calling escalated into a series of mock angry slaps. We wrestled each other onto one of the lower bunks, both of us longing to be pinned. "You kids think you invented sex," my mother was fond of saying. But hadn't we? With no instruction manual or federally enforced training period, didn't we all come away feeling we'd discovered something unspeakably modern? What produced in others a feeling of exhilaration left Jason and me with a mortifying sense of guilt. We fled the room as if, in our fumblings, we had uncapped some virus we still might escape if we ran fast enough. Had one of the counselors not caught me scaling the fence, I felt certain I could have made it back to Raleigh by morning, skittering across the surface of the ocean like one of those lizards often featured on television wildlife programs.

When discovered making out with one of the Greek bus drivers, a sixteen-year-old camper was forced to stand beside the flagpole dressed in long pants and thick sweaters. We watched her cook in the hot sun until, fully roasted, she crumpled to the pavement and passed out.

"That," the chief counselor said, "is what happens to people who play around."

If this was the punishment for a boy and a girl, I felt certain the penalty for two boys somehow involved barbed wire, a team of donkeys, and the nearest volcano. Nothing, however, could match the cruelty and humiliation Jason and I soon practiced upon each other. He started a rumor that I had stolen an athletic supporter from another camper and secretly wore it over my mouth like a surgical mask. I retaliated, claiming he had expressed a desire to become a dancer. "That's nothing," he said to the assembled crowd, "take a look at what I found on David's bed!" He reached into the pocket of his tennis shorts and withdrew a sheet of notebook paper upon which were written the words I LIKE GUYS. Presented as an indictment, the document was both pathetic and comic. Would I supposedly have written the note to remind myself of that fact, lest I forget? Had I intended to wear it taped to my back, advertising my preference the next time our rented buses carried us off to yet another swinging sexual playground?

I LIKE GUYS. He held the paper above his head, turning a slow circle so that everyone might get a chance to see. I supposed he had originally intended to plant the paper on my bunk for one of the counselors to find. Presenting it himself had foiled the note's intended effect. Rather than beating me with sticks and heavy shoes, the other boys simply groaned and looked away, wondering why he'd picked the thing up and carried it around in his pants pocket. He might as well have hoisted a glistening turd, shouting, "Look what he did!" Touching such a foul document made him suspect and guilty by association. In attempting to discredit each other, we wound up alienating ourselves even further.

Jason—even his name seemed affected. During meals I studied him from across the room. Here I was, sweating onto my plate, my stomach knotted and cramped, when *he* was the one full of shit. Clearly he had tricked me, cast a spell or slipped something into my food. I watched as he befriended a girl named Theodora and held her hand during a screening of *A Lovely Way to Die,* one of the cave paintings the head counselor offered as a weekly movie.

She wasn't a bad person, Theodora. Someday the doctors might find a way to transplant a calf's brain into a human skull, and then she'd be just as lively and intelligent as he was. I tried to find a girlfriend of my own, but my one possible candidate was sent back home when she tumbled down the steps of the Parthenon, causing serious damage to her leg brace.

Jason looked convincing enough in the company of his girlfriend. They scrambled about the various ruins, snapping each other's pictures while I hung back fuming, watching them nuzzle and coo. My jealousy stemmed from the belief that he had been cured. One fistful of my flesh and he had lost all symptoms of the disease.

Camp ended and I flew home with my legs crossed, dropping my bag of stolen souvenirs and racing to the bathroom, where I spent the next several days sitting on the toilet and studying my face in a hand mirror. *I like guys.* The words had settled themselves into my features. I was a professional now, and it showed.

I returned to my volunteer job at the mental hospital, carrying harsh Greek cigarettes as an incentive to some of the more difficult patients.

"Faggot!" a woman shouted, stooping to protect her collection of pinecones. "Get your faggoty hands away from my radio transmitters."

"Don't mind Mary Elizabeth," the orderly said. "She's crazy."

Maybe not, I thought, holding a pinecone up against my ear. She's gotten the faggot part right, so maybe she was onto something.

The moment we boarded our return flight from Kennedy to Raleigh, Lisa re-arranged her hair, dropped her accent, and turned to me saying, "Well, I thought that was very nice, how about you?" Over the course of five minutes, she had eliminated all traces of her reckless European self. Why couldn't I do the same?

In late August my class schedule arrived along with the news that I would not be bused. There had been violence in other towns and counties, trouble as far away as Boston; but in Raleigh the transition was peaceful. Not only students but many of the teachers had been shifted from one school to another. My new science teacher was a black man very adept at swishing his way across the room, mocking everyone from Albert Einstein to the dweebish host of a popular children's television program. Black and white, the teachers offered their ridicule as though it were an olive branch. "Here," they said, "this is something we each have in common, proof that we're all brothers under the skin."

CAROLINE KETTLEWELL

Auditorium

I am an infraction. Sitting in the gloom of the auditorium illuminated by the flickering images projected on the movie screen, I am guilty of holding the hand of the boy sitting next to me.

Nowhere in the rule book of the boys' boarding school where I live is it written down that a student may not hold the hand of a faculty daughter, nor has anyone ever expressly stated this rule to me. Nevertheless, I know that the heat of his flesh against mine is deemed an alarming transgression.

Therefore when the auditorium door swings open with a protesting creak from unoiled hinges, to reveal the faculty master on duty silhouetted against the bright light of the auditorium's lobby, I take advantage of the few minutes I know it will take for his eyes to adjust to the darkness to ooze down in my seat until I'm crouched on the floor, releasing the seat slowly so it doesn't bang into place on its spring-loaded hinge. I creep sideways along the row a few feet, then slither back upward into a new seat. Now no specific crime can be laid at my feet, although my mere presence in the auditorium, a mere body's length from the boy I am known to associate with, still constitutes grounds for suspicion.

In a few minutes the master will begin prowling the crowd of boys spread throughout the auditorium for this Saturday night's film, searching for contraband Coke cans and chocolate bars, the smell of chewing gum, feet propped on the back of the seat in front of them, and other harbingers of incipient anarchy. I'm a harbinger too, so I slouch down in my seat hoping the back of my head, with its long braid concealed, will look sufficiently boyish to allow me to pass without closer scrutiny. For if I'm discovered in such close proximity with the boy I was holding hands with, the boy will certainly be advised sharply to move to another row, perhaps even to leave the auditorium altogether. I can't bear the thought of his banishment, because it will be another week before we can again steal these two hours' cocoon of darkness, again skirt the edge of license.

For as long as I can remember I've lived here on this campus at the foot of the Blue Ridge Mountains, surrounded by a cast of boys that has reshaped itself every autumn. We've taken all our meals together in the same dining room, we've been on camping and hiking trips together, I've heard their names and their academic and personal travails recounted endlessly by my parents and other faculty, and yet until this fall I've hardly ever bothered to notice any one of them. A favorite baby-sitter here and there, and the rest of them nothing more than a mob of blazers and Top-Siders herded about to the school's inflexible rhythm of chapel, classes, meals, assemblies, sports, study, bed.

Then last summer I turned twelve. Now over the declining months of fall I've found myself unanticipatedly transfixed, bewildered, thrilled, and unsettled by the attentions of a handful of students three and four years older than me, boys whose strong arms and deep voices and bare, lean, muscled bodies stripped to the waist for touch football have mesmerized me into a strange trance.

I've come unexpectedly to this predicament, as though stumbling across it while on my way somewhere else. Five minutes ago I was a scruffy tomboy intent on skinned knees and derring-do; now suddenly I am Alice down the rabbit hole, without compass or map in the strange world of desire. Love is the province of women, and I, who have spent most of my life in a world defined by boys, have always found the art of being a girl mystifying and alien. All those lotions and powders and cool, coy glances, and underwear so refined it demands a French name: *lingerie*—it all feels like so much artifice, so much work, that only last summer I would have been insulted by the suggestion that any of it ever would have interested me. Now I find myself scrabbling unfamiliarly through *Seventeen* magazines and lip gloss and the steamier parts of cheap paperbacks, like a child pawing through a dress-up trunk, trying on this or that piece in the armament of girlhood with awkward, painful self-consciousness. Hoping nevertheless that the costume will win me the role—the ingenue; the love interest. The pretty girl with the perfect hair who always knows just the right so-clever thing to say.

But I have hopelessly tangled hair and hopelessly crooked teeth, and when I speak I'm generally more clever than right, so I keep suspecting that they are courting my company only because they've (wrongly) concluded that I'll put them a half step closer to their true ambition: my sister—quixotic, flamboyant, enthrallingly volatile, and fourteen.

Nevertheless, I am spellbound. Away from them, my world is lit only by dull, filtered halftones. But when I am with them—no more than a few hours altogether out of each week—I feel as though I am in the midst of a crackling, surging field of energy, like Dr. Frankenstein's laboratory, bringing me to life. I can't get enough of them.

Yet I'm supposed to want none of them.

"We don't want you spending so much time with those boys," say my parents, and the other faculty scowl at us, the boys and me, when we are hanging out together outside the school dining room after dinner trading charged innuendo and repartee.

Being twelve seems to make me old enough to be expected to behave responsibly, yet still too young to be granted the privilege of liking boys. Why do adults—who are infamously irresponsible in matters of the heart, known to cheat, lie, stray, mislead, betray; to overthrow family, career, even country, for the sake of desire—nevertheless expect children, with no experience in these matters, to greet desire's first overwhelming onslaught with levelheaded good judgment, and prudently turn our backs on it?

I've failed to live up to the expectations. In spite of the admonishments, I've imprudently fallen in love.

Instead of being fondly indulged for this first blush of girlish in-
fatuation, I find myself condemned, by adults who have known me
most of my life, in an aura of disapproval that speaks in scowling
glances, blustering coughs, the barely perceptible regretful shake of
a head. Yet no one ever says precisely what I'm doing wrong, so I'm
left to conclude that I'm somehow to blame for an unruly heart that
has surrendered itself where it ought not to. After this I will always
feel there's something shameful and unseemly about falling in love.

Nevertheless, right now it feels so giddy and amazing that even
if I could help myself, I wouldn't. I doodle his name in the margins
of my schoolbooks and imagine us walking hand in hand through
flowery meadows, like in the television ads.

In fact we walk nowhere together, and never hand in hand. We
might steal a few hours on weekends, but otherwise I see him only for
a few minutes before I leave for school in the morning, for perhaps
another twenty minutes after a supper we race through so that he and
I and his roommate and a handful of others can hang out in the administrative lobby outside the dining room, before the bell calls
them for study hall or my parents, emerging from the dining room,
demand me home.

But there are those coveted hours defined by the weekly movie,
Saturday nights and sometimes Sunday afternoons as well; somehow
we manage, week after week, never quite to be directly forbidden
each other's company—perhaps because, in the end, we've committed no certifiable crime, though we labor under constant suspicion
of unspecified sins.

His roommate is one of the student projectionists, and some
weekends we all crowd together into that narrow booth smelling of
cinder blocks and dust, noisy with the sound of the film clattering
through the projector, and cluttered with old soda cans and film can-
isters and snips of damaged celluloid. For some reason, it is the projectionist's unquestioned privilege and habit to lock the door when
he is running the movie, so when I am enclosed in that booth, I feel
as though I have vanished from the world and its expectations of me,
and I am just a girl in the limitlessly engrossing company of boys. A

sharp knock on the door of the booth, however, sends me flying up the half-dozen rungs of the steel ladder bolted to the wall, that lead to an unfinished, windowless box of a storage space over top of the booth. I crouch there while below me the projectionist leans over to open the door. My heart races.

Guilt is an ugly emotion. If it had a color, it would be a gangrenous cast. Because I can't ever pin down precisely what it is that I'm guilty of in hanging out with these boys, everything I do has become suffused with a vague quality of furtive illicitness. It's the dread I hate, the feeling that I'm forever dodging just ahead of a humiliating reprimand for a crime I won't realize I've committed. Even at night, cloistered unassailably alone in my bedroom—my homework done, teeth brushed, stereo at a mere murmur—I am guilty of *thoughts* I shouldn't have. Of the boy I'm not supposed to be in love with. Of sex, which I'm supposed to know of only in the abstract, generalized terms of health class, not in the fevered curiosity of an imagination wondering what it would be like to be touched in ways never alluded to by our textbook. With no one to share them with, I consign these thoughts to guardedly elliptical journal entries as cryptically worded as espionage communiqués lest they should fall into the wrong hands and betray me.

In the projectionist's booth, the teacher who isn't looking for me and doesn't even know I'm there pops his head around the door and stage-whispers, "It looks a little out of focus to me."

The projectionist nods noncommittally. His roommate, who was holding me wrapped in his arms only a moment ago, feigns bored disinterest. The teacher nods in turn. The door clicks shut again.

This auditorium serves as the epicenter of my erotic life; dimly lit and unoccupied except for movies and morning assemblies, it lends itself to intimacy and clandestine assignations. There are five different doorways for surreptitious entry and quick exits. The stage is draped in heavy black masking curtains, making it easy to melt silently into deep shadow. These covert operations fuel my fancies; I am Mata Hari, Natty Bumppo, Her Majesty's Secret Agent evading detection. In fact with my toys so recently abandoned that a village of Fisher-Price blocks still lies scattered across my bedroom floor, frozen in mid-story, I don't understand yet that what I'm playing now isn't a game I can choose to start over again tomorrow with a different ending.

The boy I'm mad for is seventeen, but so shy he rarely speaks—how we've managed to cross the divide of our mutual inexperience is a mystery—and I've made of this silence a blank page on which to write the story I want to read. From the bare outline I have gleaned of his life—a German orphan, birth date unknown, adopted by an American family who seem subsequently to have lost interest in him as though he were a puppy impulsively brought home from the pound and then regretted—I've cast a romantic tragedy in which I will star as redeeming love.

The life he leads in my absence—the way he folds his sweaters, the blankets on his bed, his homework assignments, the magazines he might read—feels utterly intangible. Does he raise his hand to answer questions in class? Does he shampoo with Breck or brush his teeth with Colgate? At night I stand in my bedroom window, staring across campus to the distant squares of light from the dormitories, longing to believe he's standing at his window looking for me.

No girls of any age are allowed in these dorms, and in all the years I've lived at this school I've never set foot in those hallways except in the early weeks of summer break, when industrial-size trash cans brim with broken lacrosse sticks and abandoned three-ring binders, and dust bunnies scud about beneath the stripped beds and emptied desks. A locker room funk of stale socks, blended with a treacly hint of Sugar Babys and Coca-Colas, lingers.

The terra incognita of the dorms now seems fairly to pulse with an exotic, forbidden masculinity, like some reverse purdah. Strange, liquid shouts issue along with drizzles of steam from the frosted windows of the bathrooms. Walking in studied casualness by the dorms and casting a furtive, curious eye, I catch an occasional glimpse of an arm, a head, a body silhouetted against the light from a dorm room and rendered suddenly intriguing only by the setting. I have no idea which room, which hallway is his. Any one of those half-seen figures might be him.

*   *   *

One Sunday afternoon in the cinder block womb of the empty auditorium, we cross the border of our first kiss—the two of us so equally unschooled that we huddle awkwardly against the side of the proscenium arch, arms draped gingerly across arms, dry lips pressed flat against dry lips as we have seen it in movies, each of us thinking we haven't got it right, somehow, but where have we gone wrong?

"Oh my God," says his roommate in exasperation, rolling his eyes, when we admit with coy pride to this consummation. "That's not how you kiss. I'll show you how to kiss," and under the weak yellow light of the Exit sign he wraps me in a tight embrace and snakes his tongue into my mouth. I might have pulled back, but I don't.

By midwinter, my first love hovers abandoned on the periphery while I traverse more dangerous territory with this much bolder boy, my projectionist. I plunge eagerly into the darkened auditorium, his lair. Now I'm quite clear exactly what I'm guilty of: a raw, immodest desire to know more. What's worse, I'm guilty of being unimproved by my guilt: I feel rotten; I feel that a more exemplary girl would scorn such temptations, and that doesn't stop me for a moment. I welcome his hands to wander unimpeded; I relish the taste of him and the bruising pressure of his lips; I thrill to his brazen suggestions.

To my journal, I declare I'm in love with him, but this claim is merely a sop to my conscience. In truth, though I can't admit it to myself, I'm chasing only the strange, exhilarating power I feel at the sound of his breath ragged in my ear.

Another Sunday. There's a movie playing, but it's not his week to show it, so we sit bored and blameless in the administrative lobby in the glare of daylight from the picture windows. I feel tired and used-up in that Sunday way, when the weekend is done fulfilling or failing your anticipations of it and the week has been drained to its dregs. In the unkind light of day even our usual banter of barbs and provocations rings listless; what language we truly share seems to be spoken only in darkness.

He gets up and paces restlessly. He sits down again. He slumps into the sofa, his long legs stretched out in a dispirited slouch. He sits up, then suddenly leans forward conspiratorially across the coffee table that separates us.

"Look," he says, and he begins rolling back the long sleeve of his button-down shirt. I see that the yellow broadcloth is stained in rust-brown blotches. Another roll to the sleeve and I see the first cut, still livid, a slash across the top of his forearm. We sit in complete silence as this strange striptease unfolds, both of us transfixed by the sight of his emerging arm. The cuts—perhaps half-a-dozen parallel gashes —are not deep, but they're a mess of blackened scab and oozing blood and weeping plasma.

It's not what I'm expecting, there on a still Sunday afternoon when I'm watching the way he prowls and slinks like a cat and thinking about the coiled power of his body beneath my hands. Yet I'm not horrified, alarmed, or sickened by this sudden shift. Instead, an odd, giddy excitement races through me, like an adrenaline rush, at the sight of his wounded arm. I don't need to ask him what he's done, or why. I *know*. Only a few weeks ago I have spent an afternoon in the principal's office at my own school not explaining to anyone's satisfaction what I'd been doing when I was found in the girls' bathroom trying (but not succeeding, with a blade too dull for the job) to slice open my arm with my Swiss Army knife.

It's not that I didn't want to oblige with a suitable explanation; I'm the kind of overeager, hand-waving student who covets the approval of authority figures, and what with all the behind-the-scenes (if yet undiscovered) transgressing I've lately been guilty of I figured I had a lot of lost ground to recover. But how do you expect anyone to understand the true answer: *I want to cut because I know it will make me feel better?*

Don't be absurd, they would have said first of all.

And *what could you possibly have to feel bad about?* (Without wanting to know or bothering to believe any answer, because de facto twelve-year-old girls from nice families don't have any problems but their own silly self-importance.)

And *stop trying to make yourself the center of attention,* they would have concluded.

Thus, better left unexplained.

But here, now, in my projectionist's perfectly mutilated arm, is the answer *I've* been looking for.

I raise my eyes slowly to meet his.

"Razor blade," he says.

This is his gift, his legacy to me—that three months shy of my thirteenth birthday, I find like a sigh of satisfaction that a razor blade drawn slowly over the pale curve of biceps, thigh, hip, is indeed the price of absolution. From what? Guilt, it might be, or a mounting sense of disorder, or confusion, or I'm not sure what, but my head is so full of *should* and *don't* and *stop* and *go* and *want* and *flee,* and it's gotten so hard to think straight—I just need quiet. For a day. Or an hour. Or twenty minutes. I'll take what I can get.

Bloodletting was once thought to free the body of ill humours. At school every day, when I along with the rest of my class mumble through the Lord's Prayer in the morning and grace at lunch—are we not beseeching the favor of a God who demanded blood for the expiation of our sins?

The delicate bite of steel into flesh becomes the coherent center I can understand, precise in its simplicity: blade renders blood renders silence. I delight in the neat geometry of this equation, and feel compelled to revisit it again and again. Now I can be fall and redemption all at once, embodied. I fly to my projectionist, and like Persephone I cross the threshold from bright daylight into gathering gloom, where arms reach out to draw me further into the darkness.

GLO DEANGELIS

A Conversation with Judy Blume

*F*ew writers of the past century have had such a particular and broad-reaching influence on young readers as Judy Blume. Her twenty-two books have sold more than seventy million copies and her work has been translated into twenty languages. Her classic books include: Are You There God? It's Me, Margaret; Blubber; Superfudge; Forever; and most recently, the phenomenal best-seller Summer Sisters.

Judy Blume is the 1996 recipient of the American Library Association's Margaret A. Edwards award for lifetime achievement, one of more than ninety awards she has won. She is founder and trustee of the Kids Fund, a charitable and educational foundation supported by royalties from several of her books. She also serves on the Council of the Authors Guild and is an active spokesperson for the National Coalition Against Censorship, working to protect intellectual freedom.

Glo DeAngelis interviewed Judy Blume for Tales Out of School *in the summer of 1999 at the author's home on Martha's Vineyard.*

GLO DEANGELIS: What books did you read as a child?

JUDY BLUME: My mother was a reader and she took me to the library when I was very young. I would sit on the floor and pull books off the shelves. What I really loved about them was the way they smelled. Of course I loved the pictures, too, but I never turned the pages of a book without sniffing it first. Only then would I make up

stories to go with the pictures. One day, when I was about four years
old, I found *Madeline* (by Ludwig Bemelmans). I loved that book so
much I memorized it. I thought it was the only copy of *Madeline* in
the whole world. At home I hid it, so my mother couldn't take it back
to the library. She kept asking, "Do you know where that book is?" I
knew I was being very bad, but I told her I didn't know. There was
no way I was going to part with that book. She found the book many
months later. She would have bought me my own copy of *Madeline*
had I asked, but I'd no idea then that was a possibility.

When I was in fifth grade my mother bought me the Betsy-Tacy
books by Maud Hart Lovelace. They were the first books that spoke
directly to me. I wanted to jump inside them and hang out with
Betsy and her friends. I read the Nancy Drew books, too. I bought
one a week with my allowance. But by the time I was twelve I was
into adult books. Our living room was filled with books. Nobody
ever told me what I could or couldn't read. And I loved browsing. So
I went from Nancy Drew to J. D. Salinger. Then my friends and I
found *The Fountainhead* by Ayn Rand. We certainly didn't know
what we were reading, but it was exciting to come across those racy
passages. We thought, *Oh, you can find all of this in books too!*

GD: You have a great ear for dialogue. What do you hear young
people talking about?

JB: They talk about the same things we all have on our minds.
They talk about their families, their friends, their lives at school,
which is the equivalent of an adult discussing the workplace. In their
letters they talk about how they're getting along in the world. They
question who they are and dream of what they want to do.

GD: Who do you think inspires a child to learn?

JB: Though it's tempting to say inspiration comes from the family, for many children that's not the case. If they're lucky, yes, they're
encouraged to learn by parents who value knowledge and creative
thinking. But there are a lot of self-inspired children out there, too
—remarkable children who, through their own curiosity and interests, are going to learn, no matter how bleak their family lives may
be. And some lucky children will be inspired by a teacher or teachers.
I was.

GD: Where was your high school?

JB: I went through the public schools in Elizabeth, New Jersey. We had two high schools when I was growing up, segregated by sex, the only such public high schools in the state. A thousand girls attended my school, in grades ten to twelve. (Now there's one large coed public high school in Elizabeth.) I had two inspirational teachers during those years. One was a history teacher. He treated us as intelligent young women and expected more of us than any other teacher. Though he was demanding, I found his class exhilarating. I remember thinking, *This is what it will be like next year at college.* The other taught journalism and English. He encouraged us to express ourselves without fear, by providing a warm and nurturing classroom atmosphere. He wasn't afraid to laugh with us, to enjoy us. Too many teachers don't expect enough of their students. It's not just about making demands, it's about helping students get to that other place where they're *really* thinking—not just to give a teacher the *right* answer, but thinking for themselves. Of course it's easy to sit here and discuss this in my living room. It's very different for a teacher to inspire every child when faced with twenty-five students, each of them so different. Teachers get frustrated, too. My English teacher attended our fortieth high school reunion. Many of us had the chance to tell him again what an inspiration he had been.

GD: Do you sense a missing piece in traditional American education?

JB: There is no one "traditional American education." Our schools are all over the place. So much of it is luck of the draw. Everything depends on the teachers and the schools in your community. Are you going to get that one teacher who makes a difference or are you going to go all through school thinking it's a big yawn?

Taking the fear out of education could be an important step forward. We have principals who are terrified of their school boards, so they're not going to take any chances. These are the principals who tell the teachers, "No controversial materials. We don't want to make waves. Let's not do anything that could get us in trouble with the school board or any of the parents." The teachers working with and under these principals are often afraid to take risks. Their jobs could be in jeopardy. They have families to support. Of course, many teachers take a stand anyway. They're brave and determined. They respect their students. They'll teach that *controversial* book. They'll encourage their students to think critically. They'll appreciate their students' creative efforts. And they're the ones who will continue to inspire. It will be interesting to see what evolves, what ideas will be acceptable in our schools in the coming years.

GD: How do you think the threat or perceived threat of violence is changing students' relationship with their schools?

JB: It's very scary. School should be a safe haven. Yet for some children school doesn't feel safe even if there is no threat of physical violence. For some kids, just getting up and going to school every day is traumatic. I'm talking here about the kind of emotional abuse that sometimes takes place in the classroom. School is hell for a lot of kids. Many times this has little to do with outside influences; it has to do with their peers—victimization within the classroom, horrific bullying in the halls and on the playgrounds. In the case of Columbine (High School in Littleton, Colorado), it was widely reported that bullying may have played a role. Now plenty of kids have been bullied and haven't retaliated by killing people or by trying to blow up their schools, and certainly, it's not a valid excuse for the death and destruction they caused. But I would like to see the day when bullying will not be tolerated at school. I would like to see it brought out into the open, discussed in the classroom. I'm not sure how much adults can do about such behavior once school is over for the day. Kids can be cruel. We all know that. There isn't any magic formula, but awareness helps. Victims of this abuse can be so ashamed they often don't tell their parents or any other adult. But I know, from the kids who write to me about bullying, how terrified they are. I've known kids who throw up every morning they're so dreading the day to come. It's up to the principal and teachers to set the tone within the classrooms. Usually, the worst bullying will happen under the jurisdiction of the teacher who's most oblivious.

The physical violence that's erupted in schools—the shootings we've read about and seen on TV is something else. There are no simplistic answers, though some politicians would have us believe otherwise.

GD: I'm thirty-three years old. Your books were incredibly popular while I was in school. A Judy Blume book was passed around like a dog-eared treasure, creating a community of grade school readers. How do you suppose books can do this? Create a sense of connectedness for young people, I mean?

JB: It's happening again right now with J. K. Rowling's Harry Potter books. Her books are connecting children all over the world. My grandson loves them. He'll talk about them with his friends with a passion usually reserved for *Pokémon* (the video game). I'm not sure how it happens. There's certainly no way to predict when it will happen. Every once in a while, a character or story comes along that touches children very deeply. With my books, I think it happened because kids felt that I was writing about their secret lives. Through my books I somehow let them know they weren't alone in their feelings and experiences. They assumed adults didn't know the things they were reading about in my books. I don't think they thought of me as a real adult. They thought of me as one of them. When something like this happens with a book and you're a part of it . . . well, it's just amazing.

GD: So much is being said about education by political figures and education experts, from methodology debates over how to best help emergent readers to the concern around national testing. How do you think readers are made?

JB: It starts with reading to the child. It's never too early to begin. We started reading to my grandson when he was a baby. Books were always a part of his life. His crib was filled with Board books. When he learned to read on his own he was afraid to tell us, thinking if we knew, we would no longer read to him. We had to reassure him, continuing to read every night before bed. You're never too old to listen to a good story. Good listeners make good readers. Next, take kids to the library, and even the bookstore, if you can afford it. Let them choose their own books. Try not to be judgmental about what they like to read. No reason why you can't also bring home the books you'd like to share with them. It doesn't matter if a child is reading the newspaper or the back of a cereal box. What's important is that the child is reading. Sure, we want them to read widely and probably they will, if we don't tell them what to read. It helps when kids see their parents enjoying books, too. If a child can find interest, engagement, and pleasure in reading, then, hopefully, that child will become a lifelong reader.

You mentioned the debate over national testing . . . well, if you want to get into that, you're talking to the world's worst test taker. First, let me tell you a story about a young man I know. He scored quite high on the college boards, not only because he's bright, but also because at his high school, an enormous part of the educational focus (in his junior and senior years) was on how to take the college boards—how to "beat the test." But is that really what we want to teach our kids? Is that really how we want to utilize their time in school? There must be a middle ground between preparing them to ace the boards and leaving them in a state of panic over having to take them.

The latter was my experience. When I took the college boards I'd had no preparation at all. Every word and number swam in front of me. I can remember having this sort of out-of-body experience where I saw myself running from the room. Of course, I didn't. But I couldn't focus or concentrate either. I was an A student at school but standardized tests were a nightmare for me. I looked down at the answer sheet with all those empty circles and filled them in randomly, without reading even one question. When the results came in, my guidance teacher was speechless. She told me I'd have to take the test again. But I didn't. I couldn't. I was lucky to get into college based on my high school grades, teacher recommendations, and extracurricular activities. I don't know what would happen today. I do know standardized tests can't measure our creativity. If I had been judged only by that test and nothing else—if the rest of my life depended on that test—I'd be in terrible shape now, a failure. So, from my own experience, I'm not in favor of *more* standardized tests at earlier ages. Life has more to do with looking at all aspects of a problem and using one's own creativity in finding solutions than it does with choosing someone's idea of one absolutely right answer every time.

GD: You've been interviewed a lot. Are there any questions on school you've been waiting to be asked?

JB: There is something I'd like to mention that I'm not sure I've said before. When I was starting to write, I read a little pamphlet published by the Connecticut State Board of Education called *Teach Us What We Want to Know*. That pamphlet still speaks to me, because it encourages us to teach children what they want to know, when they want to know it. A great teacher can bring any subject to life. But it's important to listen to the children, too.

FRANCESCA DELBANCO

The Progressive Basics

I was raised during the 1970s in a small town in southern Vermont, populated largely by mill workers who lived in trailers and hippies who lived in lean-tos. My parents, who didn't belong comfortably to either category, moved there from New York City to teach at the college that shares the town's name, Bennington. Life in Bennington was a bohemian affair: the town selectman played in the local orchestra, the campus green featured art installations starring students and professors in various states of undress, and the college president grew prize-winning tubers in his patch of community garden. I have a photograph of my mother and father from that era, lying next to each other in a banana-shaped hammock, wearing matching hand-woven serapes. I keep it as proof that even the sanest, most grounded people are susceptible to the occasional vogue.

Anyone who has lived in a university town knows that the prevailing ethos of campus life, whatever it may be, has a trickle-down effect on the rest of the community. There were few residents of Bennington who remained untouched by the creative, avant-garde esprit of the college—even our next-door neighbor, the town pediatrician, converted her garage into a metal-working studio and displayed her work in the waiting room of her office. It was only natural that those liberal ideals of higher learning, the educational values that made "Composition for Nonmusical Sound" and "Body Parts Art" viable concentrations at a degree-granting institution, would filter down to those of us at more elementary stages of our academic careers. When the time came for me to lace up my red Keds and hoist on my first backpack, I reported for duty to the Prospect School, a tiny private school in a three-room farmhouse that billed itself as "an experiment in progressive learning." I have often wondered, in the two decades since that day, what might prompt parents to gamble several thousand dollars and their own child's future on "an experiment."

Here are some of the disciplines on the list of educational priorities at Prospect: woodworking, painting, cooking, sewing, gardening, weaving, small worlds (blocks and dollhouses), animal rearing—practical, pioneer-inspired skills I've come to think of as the "progressive basics." The theory behind the Prospect philosophy was that students learn best when they study what interests them most. Functionally speaking, this was a very sweet deal. I was intensely interested in becoming a professional ballerina at that time, an ambition that my teacher, Dirck, encouraged wholeheartedly, though no one else seemed dazzled by my talent. Dirck seized upon my interest in dance as a natural avenue for me to learn about rhythm (progressive math), choreography (progressive composition), and physical discipline (progressive sports). For me, the main dividend was the right to wear a tutu and ballet slippers to school. Now, in a more strictly regimented environment, such clothing choices might have been discouraged as distracting or disrespectful, but freedom of expression was a cherished value at Prospect. In fact, a boy in my class wore his Halloween costume, a plastic monster mask with a built-in electronic death groan, for six straight weeks.

An average day at Prospect: you arrived in the morning and reported to your group meeting. ("Grades," naturally, were too hierarchical; group divisions were supposedly based on temperament and learning style.) After group meeting came indoor time, followed by snack, then outdoor time and, finally, free play. Alone time was also a prized elective. We were always allowed, at any given moment, to cease whatever we were doing and retreat into the "private room," a closet furnished with pillows, afghans, and an anthology of multicultural fairy tales. Of course, it would have been difficult to evaluate our performance in such abstract subjects as "Dream Sharing," so every semester the teachers sent our parents extensive written comments in lieu of assigning letter grades. (For the record, chilly personality analysis can be just as damning as a mediocre letter grade. Dirck had a way of suggesting that while I excelled in all competitive arenas, I was not the most adept sharer in group one. This critique has haunted me for the past twenty years, and in some small way I feel that I am proving myself to Dirck every time I offer up a bite of my sandwich, or a quarter to make a telephone call.)

The few rules we were required to follow (no bossing anyone around, no shouting, generous use of *please* and *thank you*) Dirck pledged to follow as well, resulting in such gently and grammatically problematic passive-aggressive statements as "Francesca, the bathroom faucet needs to be turned off." Dirck was a mild-mannered believer in absolute democracy. For every unit he taught us, we were invited to teach him something, a practice he gave a Sanskrit name which translated into English as "learning exchange." I spent a good deal of time working with him on arabesques; by the time I moved on to group two, we had worked up a graceful pas de deux.

While our brothers and sisters at Bennington Elementary School had multiplication tables drilled into their brains by rote repetition, we subjects of the Prospect experiment practiced whittling different types of wood. They memorized state capitals; we made artwork out of nonperishables from the school kitchen. They conjugated verb tenses and diagrammed sentences; we learned to feed baby goats from EvenFlo bottles. On the rare occasions where our public school and private school worlds collided, such as the annual Recreation Center Youth Athletic Tournament, we routinely got our asses kicked ("athletics" at Prospect generally required a leotard and a Philip Glass accompaniment). Anyway, competition was not valued or encouraged at our school. Wanting to win was a sign of bad character. We were content just to sit outside and sketch the different varieties of clouds hovering over the playing fields, and to pick edible clover for the next day's snack.

The party ended when I was eight years old. I don't know exactly what spawned my parents' change of heart, but I do remember sitting on my bunk bed one spring night, weaving a God's eye out of Popsicle sticks and yarn, when my mother came into my room and asked me to help her with some long division. I, of course, had never heard of division, much less long division, and what followed was an ugly scene exposing my arithmetical inadequacies. The next fall I was dressed in a kilt and a sweater vest, sitting on a school bus headed across the state border into Massachusetts, to begin my new existence as a prep school girl.

Though I was far behind my new classmates in certain basic skills (such as telling time on a nondigital clock), apparently I had learned something at Prospect, after all: I tested into the grade ahead of my age group, and the administration encouraged my parents to let me skip up. (Incidentally, this was true of the majority of my peers who left Prospect during elementary school: we were almost all invited to skip grades or join the advanced tracks at our new schools.) The transition was disorienting at first—not because of the academic demands so much as the unfamiliar environment of homework, exams, scores. But Dirck's analysis proved right: I thrived on competition, that black sin of progressivism, and fell in line quickly on the brick paths of my new school campus. I traded in my handmade journal for a college-ruled notebook, wore my hair in a ponytail, gave up ballet, and joined the field hockey team. I learned to speak French, to recite the order of the American presidents, to identify the periodic elements by their symbols, and to perform long division. Eventually I matriculated at an Ivy League college and wrote an honors thesis on the Civil War.

The Prospect School shut its doors before I finished college. Just as "the experiment" was perfectly suited to the seventies culture of free-form creativity, it was ill suited to the eighties culture of status-consciousness and demonstrable achievement. Enrollment dwindled, tuition went up, and soon the only people in our town who could afford to send their children there could also afford the fanciest private schools in New England. I felt real regret reading the alumni report that contained the news of closure. While it's easy to tally the tangible opportunities I've gained from my more "prestigious" degrees, part of me has always felt I owe the greatest debt to Prospect.

Those first years of school are formative ones, and though I can't claim to remember much about stained-glass smelting or chick incubation, I know that my confidence and desire to learn flourished under the vaguely supervisory presence of teachers like Dirck, who believed in standing back and letting us discover our own best talents.

After college, I moved to New York City and got hired as a reporter for *Seventeen,* the monthly magazine read by some 2.5 million teenage girls. The editors sized me up quickly and assigned me to the only beat that had nothing to do with fashion or beauty: a regular feature story called "School Zone." Every month, I traveled with a photographer to a different American high school, interviewed fifty or so kids, and then returned to the office to compose my article about life, school, and culture in such exotic locales as Salt Lake City and Little Rock.

What I discovered, after the initial thrill of striding through the nation's largest schools without a hall pass wore off, is that most American high schools are extraordinarily similar. One town's Mardi Gras Society may be another's Young Farm Association, but the basic curricula, activities, clubs, and social cliques don't vary all that much from place to place, at least not in a way which can be adequately conveyed in an eight-hundred-word column. That broad-spectrum continuity makes sense—after all, we have national educational standards, and national magazines like the one I work for to dictate taste and trends on a countrywide level.

But since my job was to churn out fresh copy for every issue, copy that made tenth grade life in St. Louis, Missouri, seem glamorous and intriguing and worth reading about (and also worth my first-class plane ticket and generous per diem expense account), I began to worry. Month after month, my editor slouched into my office, "School Zone" proofs and grease pencil in hand, begging for something sexier to lead with than yet another state athletic championship or outstanding A.P. program. The solution, I argued to the editor in chief when she summoned me into her office to apprise me of "School Zone"'s flagging ratings was to start profiling different kinds of schools. She looked at me doubtfully, unable to imagine a school sufficiently different from the ones we already covered to breathe life back into the ailing column. Apparently, she hadn't been to Vermont.

My own alma mater may have folded, but plenty of schools around the country still churn out enlightened, self-reliant teenagers who know how to chop firewood *and* multiply fractions, and as soon as I walked out of that meeting, I set about finding one. A short afternoon of research led me to the Putney School, a boarding academy in southern Vermont which is one of the most famous progressive schools in America. Sons and daughters of our nation's intellectual and artistic elite have been bunking in the shabby wooden cabins on the Putney campus since 1935, receiving outstanding educations both inside and outside the classroom. The public relations officer I spoke with seemed thrilled at the prospect of our story, and she sent stacks of glossy brochures featuring Putney students looking through telescopes, riding tractors, working at blackboards, slopping in cow barns, and making sculpture in the metal-working studio. The metal-working studio! Ah, youth!

I should add here that producing a "School Zone" feature—or any multiple-page spread for a commercial magazine—is an elaborate, costly endeavor. Our crews, counting producers, assistants, hairstylists, and makeup artists, never included fewer than six people, and our production budgets climbed easily to five digits every month. For these reasons, the senior members of *Seventeen*'s staff were reluctant to green-light any proposal that smacked remotely of "a gamble"; "School Zone" simply cost too much and required too much advance planning to be anything but a guaranteed hit. Which is why I prepared a particularly cogent editorial argument for Putney, emphasizing the intellectual and spiritual rewards I myself had reaped from a similar academic environment, and fervently expressing my desire to share that joy with our readers.

As our crew hauled equipment from commuter plane to rental car, across two-lane New England highways packed bumper to bumper with leaf-peeping tourists, I orated unceasingly on the merits of progressive education. Eyes may have glazed over while I sang the Prospect campfire songs, but nothing could temper my enthusiasm on the homeward-headed pilgrimage. Eventually the landscape, ablaze in its autumnal glory, dulled even the rumblings of urban dissent emanating from the backseat; so did our pit stop for apple cider at the general store in Brattleboro. Pulling up the long dirt drive to the cluster of white farmhouses and red barns on the Putney campus, I felt as if I were being reunited with a dear old friend. I leaped out of the car and went to the main building to announce our arrival. The public relations officer, our administrative contact, greeted me warmly and offered us a tour.

"I should tell you," she said, snapping her down vest as we headed back outside, "some of our students are a bit anxious about your arrival."

This was par for the course, I reassured her. Our school visits always generated a frenzy of adolescent excitement; in Chicago, our car had been surrounded by fans of the magazine hoping for a glimpse of someone famous.

She looked at me placidly. "That won't happen here."

The entrance hall of the first building she led us to, the dining complex, was plastered in pages photocopied from *Seventeen*. Scrawled across each of them, in brightly colored magic marker, were angry slogans: Seventeen Hurts Women; Take Your Superficiality Back to New York; This Magazine Is Capitalist Poison! My eyes widened.

"Something's always being protested around here," she said, waving her hand dismissively.

Inside the dining room, students stood gathered around a table, clad in white T-shirts spray-painted with the words Fuck Seventeen. Some of them had decorated their shirts very creatively indeed, with dyes and beads and interesting bits of collage—probably neat little tailoring tricks they'd learned in sewing class. They turned toward us and stared. After a few moments of mutual gaping, I asked the public relations officer if my producer and I might have a word with her, back in the foyer. We needed to know how much of the student body was against our being there.

"The freedom to express opinions is a right we take very seriously here at Putney," she explained to us in a maddeningly calm voice.

More kids in Fuck Seventeen T-shirts paraded to lunch. "Some of our students feel that your magazine's content is in conflict with their ideals. And we value open debate as one of the most fruitful methods of education."

I redefined *value* for her in the terms of the magazine industry, and asked how she suggested we get the cheerful, upbeat story she'd promised us out of a hostile crowd. Fortunately, she'd convened an all-school assembly for that night, at which time we would explain *Seventeen*'s mission to the concerned student body.

I bit my tongue. The idea of defending our jobs to a group of wealthy private schoolers caught up in adolescent Marxism would not appeal to the crew. It did not appeal to me, alleged booster of the progressive method. But there seemed to be no alternative way to proceed. We piled back into our cars and checked into our inn early. I did not call the office to report.

That evening, as kids sprawled all over the couches and floors of the main meeting room, our "open forum" on the Putney story commenced. The students voiced their concerns about fashion magazines, the familiar litany of dangers and damages such publications could inflict on girls' self-esteem. We argued back, citing our intent to include all of them, their real pictures and real words, as proof that we were interested in more than just models and celebrities. It was a debate I'd had many times before, and in truth my own feelings on this subject are more conflicted than they are resolved. But sitting on my metal folding chair that night, fielding suggestions from a bunch of self-righteous, privileged teenagers on how to make my work more palatable to their tastes, I vowed that my own children, should I ever have any, would attend military school. Faculty members beamed proudly as their intellectual progeny questioned mainstream authority, students applauded each other for sharing their thoughts and fears, and I retreated into an elaborate fantasy about the day each of them would get a first job, and have to wear a tie or panty hose and respond politely when commanded to fax out their boss's lunch reservations. The conventions of the real world, of discipline and hierarchy, do not receive much respect or regard in the progressive philosophy. The result is charming in a six-year-old who contributes her own opinion at a dinner table full of adults. It is moderately charming in a twelve-year-old who insists on making her parents observe vegetarianism because of her political beliefs. And it is patently uncharming in a group of eighteen-year-olds who do not understand that their talents at sheepshearing and tractor riding are luxuries underwritten by their parents.

We ended the assembly by promising not to harass anyone who didn't want to participate in the story, and immediately the goodwill engendered by compromise surged around the room. Over the next days, every student we approached *did* want to participate in the story—either because we'd defended our mission so articulately, or because at some level *all* teenagers, even the most staunchly antiestablishment ones, can't resist an offer to be interviewed and photographed. The result was a fabulously interesting three days on campus: we heard a choral concert, a cello recital, and a rock band practice, toured the student art galleries, watched a play rehearsal, and ate homemade meals in the dining room. And following in the tradition of the learning exchange, we made our contribution to school life, too: our photographer taught an informal clinic on portraits, the hair and makeup assistants let students groom themselves, and I milked a cow for the first time in fifteen years.

By the time we left Putney, I felt more exhausted than I had at the end of any other "School Zone." Partly that was due to the round-the-clock schedule we had to follow in order to capture boarding school life; there was no three P.M. bell to release us to the comfort of our hotel rooms. But mostly, I think, my exhaustion came from spending three straight days with a thorny, intense crowd of teenagers who questioned every choice I made, every quote I wrote down. That degree of intrusive self-confidence never wore off during our visit, and I found myself longing for a dose of the submissive, respectful treatment I was accustomed to receiving at other schools. Self-professed liberal that I am, the seeds of conservatism already blossomed in my twenty-five-year-old heart; apparently I'd spent enough years calling my own teachers "Mr." and "Mrs." to begin to see some merit in those conventions.

*   *   *

Perhaps it's inconsistent to be both an appreciative product of progressivism and a critic of it, but returning to New York to write my column, I felt exactly that way. All that focused, individual attention on each student, all those teachers believing every child who passes through their class might be the artistic or intellectual flower of the next generation, all those exhibits and performances and adult-endorsed shrines to blossoming creativity, can combine to create a class of self-important, coddled adolescents who have no idea what will hit them the minute they leave school. At the risk of sounding like a young old fogy, I do believe a certain amount of competition—even discouragement—can be healthy. I was a terrible ballerina, and while I'm grateful to Dirck for indulging my childhood hobby and boosting my fledgling confidence, I'm equally grateful to the subsequent ballet teacher who blew the whistle on my artless, clumsy form and spared me another decade of believing I could be the next Pavlova. There comes a time when kids need to know the score, need to know they deserve a C in a subject in which they don't pass muster, need to realize the world may not appreciate their poetry or science-fair projects as much as they themselves do. I only began to learn those lessons after I left Prospect but, in moderation, they have served me well. I found it alarming at Putney to meet a group of high school seniors who had been so indulged, and had so little recognition of their own privilege.

But then again, the value of all that attentive indulgence is perfectly evident: the Putney students were confident and curious and well-spoken, they had a strong sense of themselves and a strong sense of what they believed. Once I got over feeling irked by their protest, I admired the way they chose to question *Seventeen*. I've been all across the country on my "School Zone" travels; one rarely encounters teenagers who have the courage to challenge the glossy standards set by fashion magazines. More important, and perhaps more to the point, finding an *administration* that encourages those kinds of challenges is nearly impossible. At any other school I visited, an organized movement to wear profane T-shirts to class would have been squelched with the zeal of a SWAT team. For the most part, large

public schools don't have the means or resources to nurture independent thinking of that potentially inconvenient sort: classrooms are
crowded, teachers have predetermined material they have to get
through in order to meet school requirements, and the kid who
wants to take time out to ask why, or to disagree, or to approach work
from a different angle is a big pain in the ass. I have, of course, met
artistic, unconventional students—the very sort who would flourish at Putney—all over the country, and by and large, they are either
reluctantly tolerated, ignored, or, worse, harassed and treated as a
threat to institutional order. The urge to drum kids into uniformity
has gotten particularly fierce in the recent response to school violence: the rash of strictly regimented dress codes, for example, seems
to suggest that every boy in a black coat might be the next Dylan
Kliebold or Eric Harris. Big schools prize homogeneity for its conve-
nience; the best way to control a crowd is to ensure that it's a like-
minded, well-behaved one, and while that's a valuable policy for
teachers and administrators, I'm not sure how valuable it is for students. Not every child who wants to wear a black coat, or a hat, or
even a profane T-shirt, is in danger of becoming a mass murderer.
And even if he were, would forbidding such clothing choices really
be the best way to go about saving him?

The progressive system may at times veer too far in the opposite
direction, but nurturing the individual *does* deliver intellectual divi-
dends. Kids blossom when they're taught to believe their own ideas
count, that they can do more than merely regurgitate facts and ace
standardized tests. Those first few years of dancing and singing and
exploring led a disproportionate number of my classmates from
Prospect to pursue creative careers of one sort or another—which
may account for the paltry alumni contributions that doomed the
possibility of a substantial endowment. But what a gift it was, truly,
to be paid so much attention as a child, to go to school and have a
teacher want *you* to teach *him* something, to have a say in what you're
most interested in learning. A certain amount of flakiness may be the
inevitable result of such a system, but again, so many of the classrooms I've visited on my "School Zone" route suffer from the opposite: an excess of dull, tired material, an uninspired teacher droning

on and on, row after row of glassy-eyed teenagers who can't wait for the bell to ring so they can check their pagers and go to each other's houses to play video games. I read and hear constant laments for the ubiquitousness of teen culture, the hollow pastimes of our nation's youth, their lack of decent values. But mightn't it be the culture of public education that's running our schools down, at least as much as the alleged superficiality of teen culture? Huge public high schools have a ubiquitous, national culture of their own. I've seen it. It's not the best environment for producing creative and reflective young people. And it doesn't do much more than *Seventeen* to encourage individualism, intellectualism, and tolerance of difference. All kids could profit from exposure to the sort of positive, supportive, hands-on school environment that comes with the progressive philosophy. I understand now, rather better, why my own parents took a gamble on experimental education. When and if my turn comes to bet, I'd place my marker on it, too.

ABRAHAM RODRIGUEZ JR.

The Boy Without a Flag

To Ms. Linda Falcón, wherever she is

Swirls of dust danced in the beams of sunlight that came through the tall windows, the buzz of voices resounding in the stuffy auditorium. Mr. Rios stood by our Miss Colon, hovering as if waiting to catch her if she fell. His pale mouse features looked solemnly dutiful. He was a versatile man, doubling as English teacher and gym coach. He was only there because of Miss Colon's legs. She was wearing her neon pink nylons. Our favorite.

We tossed suspicious looks at the two of them. Miss Colon would smirk at Edwin and me, saying, "Hey, face front," but Mr. Rios would glare. I think he knew that we knew what he was after. We knew, because on Fridays, during our free period when we'd get to play records and eat stale pretzel sticks, we would see her way in the back by the tall windows, sitting up on a radiator like a schoolgirl. There would be a strange pinkness on her high cheekbones, and there was Mr. Rios, sitting beside her, playing with her hand. Her face, so thin and girlish, would blush. From then on, her eyes, very close together like a cartoon rendition of a beaver's, would avoid us.

Miss Colon was hardly discreet about her affairs. Edwin had first tipped me off about her love life after one of his lunchtime jaunts through the empty hallways. He would chase girls and toss wet bathroom napkins into classrooms where kids in the lower grades sat, trapped. He claimed to have seen Miss Colon slip into a steward's closet with Mr. Rios and to have heard all manner of sounds through the thick wooden door, which was locked (he tried it). He had told half the class before the day was out, the boys sniggering behind grimy hands, the girls shocked because Miss Colon was married, so married that she even brought the poor unfortunate in one morning as a kind of show-and-tell guest. He was an untidy dark-skinned Puerto Rican type in a colorful dashiki. He carried a paper bag that smelled like glue. His eyes seemed sleepy, his Afro an uncombed Brillo pad. He talked about protest marches, the sixties, the importance of an education. Then he embarrassed Miss Colon greatly by disappearing into the coat closet and falling asleep there. The girls, remembering him, softened their attitude toward her indiscretions, defending her violently. "Face it," one of them blurted out when Edwin began a new series of Miss Colon tales, "she married a bum and needs to find true love."

"She's a slut, and I'm gonna draw a comic book about her," Edwin said, hushing when she walked in through the door. That afternoon, he showed me the first sketches of what would later become a very popular comic book entitled "Slut at the Head of the Class." Edwin could draw really well, but his stories were terrible, so I volunteered to do the writing. In no time at all, we had three issues circulating under desks and hidden in notebooks all over the school. Edwin secretly ran off close to a hundred copies on a copy machine in the main office after school. It always amazed me how copies of our comic kept popping up in the unlikeliest places. I saw them on radiators in the auditorium, on benches in the gym, tacked up on bulletin boards. There were even some in the teachers' lounge, which I spotted one day while running an errand for Miss Colon. Seeing it, however, in the hands of Miss Marti, the pig-faced assistant principal, nearly made me puke up my lunch. Good thing our names weren't on it.

It was a miracle no one snitched on us during the ensuing investigation, since only a blind fool couldn't see our involvement in the thing. No bloody purge followed, but there was enough fear in both of us to kill the desire to continue our publishing venture. Miss Marti, a woman with a battlefield face and constant odor of Chiclets, made a forceful threat about finding the culprits while holding up the second issue, the one with the hand-colored cover. No one moved. The auditorium grew silent. We meditated on the sound of a small plane flying by, its engines rattling the windows. I think we wished we were on it.

It was in the auditorium that the trouble first began. We had all settled into our seats, fidgeting like tiny burrowing animals, when there was a general call for quiet. Miss Marti, up on stage, had a stare that could make any squirming fool sweat. She was a gruff, nasty woman who never smiled without seeming sadistic.

Mr. Rios was at his spot beside Miss Colon, his hands clasped behind his back as if he needed to restrain them. He seemed to whisper to her. Soft, mushy things. Edwin would watch them from his seat beside me, giving me the details, his shiny face looking worried. He always seemed sweaty, his fingers kind of damp.

"I toldju, I saw um holdin hands," he said. "An now lookit him, he's whispering sweet shits inta huh ear."

He quieted down when he noticed Miss Marti's evil eye sweeping over us like a prison-camp searchlight. There was silence. In her best military bark, Miss Marti ordered everyone to stand. Two lone, pathetic kids, dragooned by some unseen force, slowly came down the center aisle, each bearing a huge flag on a thick wooden pole. All I could make out was that great star-spangled unfurling, twitching thing that looked like it would fall as it approached over all those bored young heads. The Puerto Rican flag walked beside it, looking smaller and less confident. It clung to its pole.

"The Pledge," Miss Marti roared, putting her hand over the spot where her heart was rumored to be.

That's when I heard my father talking.

He was sitting on his bed, yelling about Chile, about what the CIA had done there. I was standing opposite him in my dingy Pro Keds. I knew about politics. I was eleven when I read William Shirer's book on Hitler. I was ready.

"All this country does is abuse Hispanic nations," my father said, turning a page of his *Post,* "tie them down, make them dependent. It says democracy with one hand while it protects and feeds fascist dictatorships with the other." His eyes blazed with a strange fire. I sat on the bed, on part of his *Post,* transfixed by his oratorical mastery. He had mentioned political things before, but not like this, not with such fiery conviction. I thought maybe it had to do with my reading Shirer. Maybe he had seen me reading that fat book and figured I was ready for real politics.

Using the knowledge I gained from the book, I defended the Americans. What fascism was he talking about, anyway? I knew we had stopped Hitler. That was a big deal, something to be proud of.

"Come out of fairy-tale land," he said scornfully. "Do you know what imperialism is?"

I didn't really, no.

"Well, why don't you read about that? Why don't you read about Juan Bosch and Allende, men who died fighting imperialism? They stood up against American big business. You should read about that instead of this crap about Hitler."

"But I like reading about Hitler," I said, feeling a little spurned. I didn't even mention that my fascination with Adolf led to my writing a biography of him, a book report one hundred and fifty pages long. It got an A-plus. Miss Colon stapled it to the bulletin board right outside the classroom, where it was promptly stolen.

"So, what makes you want to be a writer?" Miss Colon asked me quietly one day, when Edwin and I, always the helpful ones, volunteered to assist her in getting the classroom spiffed up for a Halloween party.

"I don't know. I guess my father," I replied, fiddling with plastic pumpkins self-consciously while images of my father began parading through my mind.

When I think back to my earliest image of my father, it is one of him sitting behind a huge rented typewriter, his fingers clacking away. He was a frustrated poet, radio announcer, and even stage actor. He had sent for diplomas from fly-by-night companies. He took acting lessons, went into broadcasting, even ended up on the ground floor of what is now Spanish radio, but his family talked him out of all of it. "You should find yourself real work, something substantial," they said, so he did. He dropped all those dreams that were never encouraged by anyone else and got a job at a Nedick's on Third Avenue. My pop the counterman.

Despite that, he kept writing. He recited his poetry into a huge reel-to-reel tape deck that he had, then he'd play it back and sit like a critic, brow furrowed, fingers stroking his lips. He would record strange sounds and play them back to me at outrageous speeds, until I believed that there were tiny people living inside the machine. I used to stand by him and watch him type, his black pompadour spilling over his forehead. There was energy pulsating all around him, and I wanted a part of it.

I was five years old when I first sat in his chair at the kitchen table and began pushing down keys, watching the letters magically appear on the page. I was entranced. My fascination with the typewriter began at that point. By the time I was ten, I was writing war stories, tales of pain and pathos culled from the piles of comic books I devoured. I wrote unreadable novels. With illustrations. My father wasn't impressed. I guess he was hard to impress. My terrific grades did not faze him, nor the fact that I was reading books as fat as milk crates. My unreadable novels piled up. I brought them to him at night to see if he would read them, but after a week of waiting I found them thrown in the bedroom closet, unread. I felt hurt and rejected, despite my mother's kind words. "He's just too busy to read them," she said to me one night when I mentioned it to her. He never brought them up, even when I quietly took them out of the closet one day or when he'd see me furiously hammering on one of his rented machines. I would tell him I wanted to be a writer, and he would smile sadly and pat my head, without a word.

"You have to find something serious to do with your life," he told me one night, after I had shown him my first play, eighty pages long. What was it I had read that got me into writing a play? Was it Arthur Miller? Oscar Wilde? I don't remember, but I recall my determination to write a truly marvelous play about combat because there didn't seem to be any around.

"This is fun as a hobby," my father said, "but you can't get serious about this." His demeanor spoke volumes, but I couldn't stop writing. Novels, I called them, starting a new one every three days. The world was a blank page waiting for my words to recreate it, while the real world remained cold and lonely. My schoolmates didn't understand any of it, and because of the fat books I carried around, I was held in some fear. After all, what kid in his right mind would read a book if it wasn't assigned? I was sick of kids coming up to me and saying, "Gaw, lookit tha fat book. Ya teacha make ya read tha?" (No, I'm just reading it.) The kids would look at me as if I had just crawled out of a sewer. "Ya crazy, man." My father seemed to share that opinion. Only my teachers understood and encouraged my reading, but my father seemed to want something else from me.

Now, he treated me like an idiot for not knowing what imperialism was. He berated my books and one night handed me a copy of a book about Albizu Campos, the Puerto Rican revolutionary. I read it through in two sittings.

"Some of it seems true," I said.

"Some of it?" my father asked incredulously. "After what they did to him, you can sit there and act like a Yankee flag-waver?"

I watched the Yankee flag making its way up to the stage over indifferent heads, my father's scowling face haunting me, his words resounding in my head.

"Let me tell you something," my father sneered. "In school, all they do is talk about George Washington, right? The first president? The father of democracy? Well, he had slaves. We had our own Washington, and ours had real teeth."

As Old Glory reached the stage, a general clatter ensued.

"We had our own revolution," my father said, "and the United States crushed it with the flick of a pinkie."

Miss Marti barked her royal command. Everyone rose up to salute the flag.

Except me. I didn't get up. I sat in my creaking seat, hands on my knees. A girl behind me tapped me on the back. "Come on, stupid, get up." There was a trace of concern in her voice. I didn't move.

Miss Colon appeared. She leaned over, shaking me gently. "Are you sick? Are you okay?" Her soft hair fell over my neck like a blanket.

"No," I replied.

"What's wrong?" she asked, her face growing stern. I was beginning to feel claustrophobic, what with everyone standing all around me, bodies like walls. My friend Edwin, hand on his heart, watched from the corner of his eye. He almost looked envious, as if he wished he had thought of it. Murmuring voices around me began reciting the Pledge while Mr. Rios appeared, commandingly grabbing me by the shoulder and pulling me out of my seat into the aisle. Miss Colon was beside him, looking a little apprehensive.

"What is wrong with you?" he asked angrily. "You know you're supposed to stand up for the Pledge! Are you religious?"

"No," I said.

"Then what?"

"I'm not saluting that flag," I said.

"What?"

"I said, I'm not saluting that flag."

"Why the . . . ?" He calmed himself; a look of concern flashed over Miss Colon's face. "Why not?"

"Because I'm Puerto Rican. I ain't no American. And I'm not no Yankee flag-waver."

"You're supposed to salute the flag," he said angrily, shoving one of his fat fingers in my face. "You're not supposed to make up your own mind about it. You're supposed to do as you are told."

"I thought I was free," I said, looking at him and at Miss Colon.

"You are," Miss Colon said feebly. "That's why you should salute the flag."

"But shouldn't I do what I feel is right?"

"You should do what you are told!" Mr. Rios yelled into my face. "I'm not playing no games with you, mister. You hear that music? That's the anthem. Now you go stand over there and put your hand over your heart." He made as if to grab my hand, but I pulled away.

"No!" I said sharply. "I'm not saluting that crummy flag! And you can't make me, either. There's nothing you can do about it."

"Oh yeah?" Mr. Rios roared. "We'll see about that!"

"Have you gone crazy?" Miss Colon asked as he led me away by the arm, down the hallway, where I could still hear the strains of the anthem. He walked me briskly into the principal's office and stuck me in a corner.

"You stand there for the rest of the day and see how you feel about it," he said viciously. "Don't even think of moving from that spot!"

I stood there for close to two hours or so. The principal came and went, not even saying hi or hey or anything, as if finding kids in the corners of his office was a common occurrence. I could hear him talking on the phone, scribbling on pads, talking to his secretary. At one point I heard Mr. Rios outside in the main office.

"Some smart-ass. I stuck him in the corner. Thinks he can pull that shit. The kid's got no respect, man. I should get the chance to teach him some."

"Children today have no respect," I heard Miss Marti's reptile voice say as she approached, heels clacking like gunshots. "It has to be forced upon them."

She was in the room. She didn't say a word to the principal, who was on the phone. She walked right over to me. I could hear my heart beating in my ears as her shadow fell over me. Godzilla over Tokyo.

"Well, have you learned your lesson yet?" she asked, turning me from the wall with a finger on my shoulder. I stared at her without replying. My face burned, red hot. I hated it.

"You think you're pretty important, don't you? Well, let me tell you, you're nothing. You're not worth a damn. You're just a snotty-nosed little kid with a lot of stupid ideas." Her eyes bored holes through me, searing my flesh. I felt as if I were going to cry. I fought the urge. Tears rolled down my face anyway. They made her smile, her chapped lips twisting upwards like the mouth of a lizard.

"See? You're a little baby. You don't know anything, but you'd better learn your place." She pointed a finger in my face. "You do as you're told if you don't want big trouble. Now go back to class."

Her eyes continued to stab at me. I looked past her and saw Edwin waiting by the office door for me. I walked past her, wiping at my face. I could feel her eyes on me still, even as we walked up the stairs to the classroom. It was close to three already, and the skies outside the grated windows were cloudy.

"Man," Edwin said to me as we reached our floor, "I think you're crazy."

The classroom was abuzz with activity when I got there. Kids were chattering, getting their windbreakers from the closet, slamming their chairs up on their desks, filled with the euphoria of soon-home. I walked quietly over to my desk and took out my books. The other kids looked at me as if I were a ghost.

I went through the motions like a robot. When we got downstairs to the door, Miss Colon, dismissing the class, pulled me aside, her face compassionate and warm. She squeezed my hand.

"Are you okay?"

I nodded.

"That was a really crazy stunt there. Where did you get such an idea?"

I stared at her black flats. She was wearing tan panty hose and a black miniskirt. I saw Mr. Rios approaching with his class.

"I have to go," I said, and split, running into the frigid breezes and the silver sunshine.

At home, I lay on the floor of our living room, tapping my open notebook with the tip of my pen while the Beatles blared from my father's stereo. I felt humiliated and alone. Miss Marti's reptile face kept appearing in my notebook, her voice intoning, "Let me tell you, you're nothing." Yeah, right. Just what horrible hole did she crawl out of? Were those people really Puerto Ricans? Why should a Puerto Rican salute an American flag?

I put the question to my father, strolling into his bedroom, a tiny M-1 rifle that belonged to my G.I. Joe strapped to my thumb.

"Why?" he asked, loosening the reading glasses that were perched on his nose, his newspaper sprawled open on the bed before him, his cigarette streaming blue smoke. "Because we are owned, like cattle. And because nobody has any pride in their culture to stand up for it."

I pondered those words, feeling as if I were being encouraged, but I didn't dare tell him. I wanted to believe what I had done was a brave and noble thing, but somehow I feared his reaction. I never could impress him with my grades, or my writing. This flag thing would probably upset him. Maybe he, too, would think I was crazy, disrespectful, a "smart-ass" who didn't know his place. I feared that, feared my father saying to me, in a reptile voice, "Let me tell you, you're nothing."

I suited up my G.I. Joe for combat, slipping on his helmet, strapping on his field pack. I fixed the bayonet to his rifle, sticking it in his clutching hands so he seemed ready to fire. "A man's gotta do what a man's gotta do." Was that John Wayne? I don't know who it was, but I did what I had to do, still not telling my father. The following week, in the auditorium, I did it again. This time, everyone noticed. The whole place fell into a weird hush as Mr. Rios screamed at me.

I ended up in my corner again, this time getting a prolonged, pensive stare from the principal before I was made to stare at the wall for two more hours. My mind zoomed past my surroundings. In one strange vision, I saw my crony Edwin climbing up Miss Colon's curvy legs, giving me every detail of what he saw.

"Why?" Miss Colon asked frantically. "This time you don't leave until you tell me why." She was holding me by the arm, masses of kids flying by, happy blurs that faded into the sunlight outside the door.

"Because I'm Puerto Rican, not American," I blurted out in a weary torrent. "That makes sense, don't it?"

"So am I," she said, "but we're in America!" She smiled. "Don't you think you could make some kind of compromise?" She tilted her head to one side and said, "Aw, c'mon," in a little-girl whisper.

"What about standing up for what you believe in? Doesn't that matter? You used to talk to us about Kent State and protesting. You said those kids died because they believed in freedom, right? Well, I feel like them now. I wanna make a stand."

She sighed with evident aggravation. She caressed my hair. For a moment, I thought she was going to kiss me. She was going to say something, but just as her pretty lips parted, I caught Mr. Rios approaching.

"I don't wanna see him," I said, pulling away.

"No, wait," she said gently.

"He's gonna deck me," I said to her.

"No, he's not," Miss Colon said, as if challenging him, her eyes taking him in as he stood beside her.

"No, I'm not," he said. "Listen here. Miss Colon was talking to me about you, and I agree with her." He looked like a nervous little boy in front of the class, making his report. "You have a lot of guts. Still, there are rules here. I'm willing to make a deal with you. You go home and think about this. Tomorrow I'll come see you." I looked at him skeptically, and he added, "to talk."

"I'm not changing my mind," I said. Miss Colon exhaled painfully.

"If you don't, it's out of my hands." He frowned and looked at her. She shook her head, as if she were upset with him.

I reread the book about Albizu. I didn't sleep a wink that night. I didn't tell my father a word, even though I almost burst from the effort. At night, alone in my bed, images attacked me. I saw Miss Marti and Mr. Rios debating Albizu Campos. I saw him in a wheelchair with a flag draped over his body like a holy robe. They would not do that to me. They were bound to break me the way Albizu was broken, not by young smiling American troops bearing chocolate bars, but by conniving, double-dealing, self-serving Puerto Rican landowners and their ilk, who dared say they were the future. They spoke of dignity and democracy while teaching Puerto Ricans how to cling to the great coat of that powerful northern neighbor. Puerto Rico, the shining star, the great lapdog of the Caribbean. I saw my father, the Nationalist hero, screaming from his podium, his great oration stirring everyone around him to acts of bravery. There was a shining arrogance in his eyes as he stared out over the sea of faces mouthing his name, a sparkling audacity that invited and incited. There didn't seem to be fear anywhere in him, only the urge to rush to the attack, with his armband and revolutionary tunic. I stared up at him, transfixed. I stood by the podium, his personal adjutant, while his voice rang through the stadium. "We are not, nor will we ever be, Yankee flag-wavers!" The roar that followed drowned out the whole world.

The following day, I sat in my seat, ignoring Miss Colon as she neatly drew triangles on the board with the help of plastic stencils. She was using colored chalk, her favorite. Edwin, sitting beside me, was beaning girls with spitballs that he fired through his hollowed-out Bic pen. They didn't cry out. They simply enlisted the help of a girl named Gloria who sat a few desks behind him. She very skillfully nailed him with a thick wad of gum. It stayed in his hair until Edwin finally went running to Miss Colon. She used her huge teacher's scissors. I couldn't stand it. They all seemed trapped in a world of trivial things, while I swam in a mire of oppression. I walked through lunch as if in a trance, a prisoner on death row waiting for the heavy steps of his executioners. I watched Edwin lick at his regulation cafeteria ice cream, sandwiched between two sheets of paper. I was once like him, laughing and joking, lining up for a stickball game in the yard without a care. Now it all seemed lost to me, as if my youth had been burned out of me by a book.

Shortly after lunch, Mr. Rios appeared. He talked to Miss Colon for a while by the door as the room filled with a bubbling murmur. Then, he motioned for me. I walked through the sudden silence as if in slow motion.

"Well," he said to me as I stood in the cool hallway, "have you thought about this?"

"Yeah," I said, once again seeing my father on the podium, his voice thundering.

"And?"

"I'm not saluting that flag."

Miss Colon fell against the doorjamb as if exhausted. Exasperation passed over Mr. Rios' rodent features.

"I thought you said you'd think about it," he thundered.

"I did. I decided I was right."

"*You* were right?" Mr. Rios was losing his patience. I stood calmly by the wall.

"I told you," Miss Colon whispered to him.

"Listen," he said, ignoring her, "have you heard the story of the man who had no country?"

I stared at him.

"Well? Have you?"

"No," I answered sharply; his mouse eyes almost crossed with anger at my insolence. "Some stupid fairy tale ain't gonna change my mind anyway. You're treating me like I'm stupid, and I'm not."

"Stop acting like you're some mature adult! You're not. You're just a puny kid."

"Well, this puny kid still ain't gonna salute that flag."

"You were born here," Miss Colon interjected patiently, trying to calm us both down. "Don't you think you at least owe this country some respect? At least?"

"I had no choice about where I was born. And I was born poor."

"So what?" Mr. Rios screamed. "There are plenty of poor people who respect the flag. Look around you, dammit! You see any rich people here? I'm not rich either!" He tugged on my arm. "This country takes care of Puerto Rico, don't you see that? Don't you know anything about politics?"

"Do you know what imperialism is?"

The two of them stared at each other.

"I don't believe you," Mr. Rios murmured.

"Puerto Rico is a colony," I said, a direct quote of Albizu's. "Why I gotta respect that?"

Miss Colon stared at me with her black saucer eyes, a slight trace of a grin on her features. It encouraged me. In that one moment, I felt strong, suddenly aware of my territory and my knowledge of it. I no longer felt like a boy but some kind of soldier, my bayonet stained with the blood of my enemy. There was no doubt about it. Mr. Rios was the enemy, and I was beating him. The more he tried to treat me like a child, the more defiant I became, his arguments falling like twisted armor. He shut his eyes and pressed the bridge of his nose.

"You're out of my hands," he said.

Miss Colon gave me a sympathetic look before she vanished into the classroom again. Mr. Rios led me downstairs without another word. His face was completely red. I expected to be put in my corner again, but this time Mr. Rios sat me down in the leather chair facing the principal's desk. He stepped outside, and I could hear the familiar clack-clack that could only belong to Miss Marti's reptile legs.

They were talking in whispers. I expected her to come in at any moment, but the principal walked in instead. He came in quietly, holding a folder in his hand. His soft brown eyes and beard made him look compassionate, rounded cheeks making him seem friendly. His desk plate solemnly stated: Mr. Sepulveda, PRINCIPAL. He fell into his seat rather unceremoniously, opened the folder, and crossed his hands over it.

"Well, well, well," he said softly, with a tight-lipped grin. "You've created quite a stir, young man." It sounded to me like movie dialogue.

"First of all, let me say I know about you. I have your record right here, and everything in it is very impressive. Good grades, good attitude, your teachers all have adored you. But I wonder if maybe this hasn't gone to your head? Because everything is going for you here, and you're throwing it all away."

He leaned back in his chair. "We have rules, all of us. There are rules even I must live by. People who don't obey them get disciplined. This will all go on your record, and a pretty good one you've had so far. Why ruin it? This'll follow you for life. You don't want to end up losing a good job opportunity in government or in the armed forces because as a child you indulged your imagination and refused to salute the flag? I know you can't see how childish it all is now, but you must see it, and because you're smarter than most, I'll put it to you in terms you can understand.

"To me, this is a simple case of rules and regulations. Someday, when you're older," he paused here, obviously amused by the sound of his own voice, "you can go to rallies and protest marches and express your rebellious tendencies. But right now, you are a minor, under this school's jurisdiction. That means you follow the rules, no matter what you think of them. You can join the Young Lords later."

I stared at him, overwhelmed by his huge desk, his pompous mannerisms and status. I would agree with everything, I felt, and then, the following week, I would refuse once again. I would fight him then, even though he hadn't tried to humiliate me or insult my intelligence. I would continue to fight, until I . . .

"I spoke with your father," he said.

I started. "My father?" Vague images and hopes flared through my mind briefly.

"Yes. I talked to him at length. He agrees with me that you've gotten a little out of hand."

My blood reversed direction in my veins. I felt as if I were going to collapse. I gripped the armrests of my chair. There was no way this could be true, no way at all! My father was supposed to ride in like the cavalry, not abandon me to the enemy! I pressed my wet eyes with my fingers. It must be a lie.

"He blames himself for your behavior," the principal said. "He's already here," Mr. Rios said from the door, motioning my father inside. Seeing him wearing his black weather-beaten trench coat almost asphyxiated me. His eyes, red with concern, pulled at me painfully. He came over to me first while the principal rose slightly, as if greeting a head of state. There was a look of dread on my father's face as he looked at me. He seemed utterly lost.

"Mr. Sepulveda," he said, "I never thought a thing like this could happen. My wife and I try to bring him up right. We encourage him to read and write and everything. But you know, this is a shock."

"It's not that terrible, Mr. Rodriguez. You've done very well with him, he's an intelligent boy. He just needs to learn how important obedience is."

"Yes," my father said, turning to me, "yes, you have to obey the rules. You can't do this. It's wrong." He looked at me grimly, as if working on a math problem. One of his hands caressed my head.

There were more words, in Spanish now, but I didn't hear them. I felt like I was falling down a hole. My father, my creator, renouncing his creation, repentant. Not an ounce of him seemed prepared to stand up for me, to shield me from attack. My tears made all the faces around me melt.

"So you see," the principal said to me as I rose, my father clutching me to him, "if you ever do this again, you will be hurting your father as well as yourself."

I hated myself. I wiped at my face desperately, trying not to make a spectacle of myself. I was just a kid, a tiny kid. Who in the hell did

I think I was? I'd have to wait until I was older, like my father, in order to have "convictions."

"I don't want to see you in here again, okay?" the principal said sternly. I nodded dumbly, my father's arm around me as he escorted me through the front office to the door that led to the hallway, where a multitude of children's voices echoed up and down its length like tolling bells.

"Are you crazy?" my father half whispered to me in Spanish as we stood there. "Do you know how embarrassing this all is? I didn't think you were this stupid. Don't you know anything about dignity, about respect? How could you make a spectacle of yourself? Now you make us all look stupid."

He quieted down as Mr. Rios came over to take me back to class. My father gave me a squeeze and told me he'd see me at home. Then, I walked with a somber Mr. Rios, who oddly wrapped an arm around me all the way back to the classroom.

"Here you go," he said softly as I entered the classroom, and everything fell quiet. I stepped in and walked to my seat without looking at anyone. My cheeks were still damp, my eyes red. I looked like I had been tortured. Edwin stared at me, then he pressed my hand under the table.

"I thought you were dead," he whispered.

Miss Colon threw me worried glances all through the remainder of the class. I wasn't paying attention. I took out my notebook, but my strength ebbed away. I just put my head on the desk and shut my eyes, reliving my father's betrayal. If what I did was so bad, why did I feel more ashamed of him than I did of myself? His words, once so rich and vibrant, now fell to the floor, leaves from a dead tree.

At the end of the class, Miss Colon ordered me to stay after school. She got Mr. Rios to take the class down along with his, and she stayed with me in the darkened room. She shut the door on all the exuberant hallway noise and sat down on Edwin's desk, beside me, her black pumps on his seat.

"Are you okay?" she asked softly, grasping my arm. I told her everything, especially about my father's betrayal. I thought he would be the cavalry, but he was just a coward.

"Tss. Don't be so hard on your father," she said. "He's only trying to do what's best for you."

"And how's this the best for me?" I asked, my voice growing hoarse with hurt.

"I know it's hard for you to understand, but he really was trying to take care of you."

I stared at the blackboard.

"He doesn't understand me," I said, wiping my eyes.

"You'll forget," she whispered.

"No, I won't. I'll remember every time I see that flag. I'll see it and think, 'My father doesn't understand me.'"

Miss Colon sighed deeply. Her fingers were warm on my head, stroking my hair. She gave me a kiss on the cheek. She walked me downstairs, pausing by the doorway. Scores of screaming, laughing kids brushed past us.

"If it's any consolation, I'm on your side," she said, squeezing my arm. I smiled at her, warmth spreading through me. "Go home and listen to the Beatles," she added with a grin.

I stepped out into the sunshine, came down the white stone steps, and stood on the sidewalk. I stared at the towering school building, white and perfect in the sun, indomitable. Across the street, the dingy row of tattered uneven tenements where I lived. I thought of my father. Her words made me feel sorry for him, but I felt sorrier for myself. I couldn't understand back then about a father's love and what a father might give to insure his son safe transit. He had already navigated treacherous waters and now couldn't have me rock the boat. I still had to learn that he had made peace with The Enemy, that The Enemy was already in us. Like the flag I must salute, we were inseparable, yet his compromise made me feel ashamed and defeated. Then I knew I had to find my own peace, away from the bondage of obedience. I had to accept that flag, and my father, someone I would love forever, even if at times to my young, feeble mind he seemed a little imperfect.

MICHAEL PATRICK MACDONALD

Fight the Power

'Twas on a dreary Thursday morn'
As the buses rolled along.
They came up to our peaceful town
With orders from The Law:
Desegregate and integrate
Or you will pay the price
Of loss of pride, humility,
And even your children's lives.

But Southie's spirit was so strong,
They made us a barrack town.
They took their horses, dogs, and guns
And set them on the crowd.
The TPF, their sticks did crack
On the young and old alike.
But united still, our spirits high,
We'll fight for freedom's right.

—Helen King

M a's tunes on the accordion started to be all about the busing. She played them at rallies, sit-ins, and fundraisers for the struggle, all over Southie. The songs sounded like a lot of the Irish rebel songs we grew up with. They had the same tunes, but the words had changed: "So come on Southie, head on high / They'll never take our pride. . . ." The Black and Tans, the murderous regiments who'd wreaked havoc on Ireland on behalf of the English Crown, became the TPF (Tactical Police Force), the special force that was turning our town into a police state. The Queen of England was gone from Ma's songs too, her place taken by Judge Garrity, the federal judge who'd mandated busing, "the law of the land": "Judge Garrity and traitors too / We've just begun to fight." Garrity had an Irish name, which made it all the worse, as the Irish hated nothing more than a traitor. That's why we hated Ted Kennedy; he'd sided with the busing too, and was seen as the biggest traitor of all, being from the most important Irish family in America.

The English themselves weren't completely absent from our struggle, though. They ran the *Boston Globe* and were behind the whole thing. My friends and I started stealing stacks of the *Globe* left outside supermarkets in the early mornings. We could sell them for a dime to people on their way to work, who'd have been paying a quarter if it weren't for us. That's when I found out the *Globe* was the enemy. We tried to sell it in Southie, but too many people said they wouldn't read that liberal piece of trash if it was free, that it was to blame for the busing, with all its attacks on South Boston. I heard a few people say it was a communist paper. "Not only are they communists, they're the rich English, keeping up their hate for the Irish and Southie," Coley told me. He showed me the names of the *Globe's* owners and editors: "Winship, Taylor. All WASPs," he said, "White Anglo Saxon Protestants, forever gettin' back at the Irish for chasing them out of Boston."

Boy, was I confused now that the English were involved. We'd always hated the English for what they did to the Irish. But whatever that was, listening to Ma's Irish songs, I'd thought it was in the past and across a great big ocean. Now it was right here in Southie. I was glad to be doing my part anyway, stealing the *Boston Globe* and making a couple bucks on their loss. The rich English liberal communist bastards!

*   *   *

That September, Ma let us skip the first week of school. The whole neighborhood was boycotting school. City Councilor Louise Day Hicks and her bodyguard with the bullhorn, Jimmy Kelly, were telling people to keep their kids home. It was supposed to be just the high school kids boycotting, but we all wanted to show our loyalty to the neighborhood. I was meant to be starting the third grade at St. Augustine's School. Ma had enrolled Kevin and Kathy in the sixth and seventh grades there as well. Frankie was going to Southie High, and Mary and Joe were being sent to mostly black Roxbury, so they really had something to boycott. But on the first day, Kevin and Kathy begged Ma not to send them. "C'mon Ma, please?" I piped in. It was still warm outside and we wanted to join the crowds that were just then lining the streets to watch the busloads of black kids come into Southie. The excitement built as police helicopters hovered just above our third-floor windows, police in riot gear stood guard on the rooftops of Old Colony, and the national news camped out on every corner. Ma said okay, and we ran up to Darius Court, along the busing route, where in simpler times we'd watched the neighborhood St. Paddy's Day parade.

The whole neighborhood was out. Even the mothers from the stoop made it to Darius Court, nightgowns and all. Mrs. Coyne, up on the rooftop in her housedress, got arrested before the buses even started rolling through the neighborhood. Everyone knew she was a little soft, and I thought the excitement that day must have been a bit too much for her. She ran up to the roof and called the police "nigger lovers" and "traders," and started dancing and singing James Brown songs. "Say it loud, I'm black and I'm proud!" She nearly fell off the roof before one cop grabbed her from behind and restrained her. Everyone was laughing at that one: big fat Mrs. Coyne rolling around on the rooftop kicking and screaming, with a cop in full riot gear on top of her. Little disturbances like that broke out here and there, but most people were too intent on seeing the buses roll to do anything that might get them carted away.

I looked up the road and saw a squadron of police motorcycles speeding down Dorchester Street, right along the curb, as if they would run over anyone who wasn't on the sidewalk. The buses were coming. Police sirens wailed as hundreds of cops on motorcycles aimed at the crowds of mothers and kids, to clear the way for the law of the land. "Bacon . . . I smell bacon!" a few people yelled, sniffing at the cops. I knew that meant the cops were pigs. As the motorcycles came closer I fought to get back onto the sidewalk, but it was too crowded. I ran further into the road to avoid one motorcycle, when two more came at me from the middle of the street. I had to run across to the other side of the road, where the crowd quickly cleared a space for me on the sidewalk. All the adults welcomed me, patting me on the shoulder. "Are you all right?" "Those pricks would even kill a kid." "Pigs!" someone else shouted. I thought I'd lost Kevin and Kathy, but just then I saw them sitting on top of a mailbox up the street for a good view of the buses. They waved to me, laughing because they'd seen me almost get run over.

The road was cleared, and the buses rolled slowly. We saw a line of yellow buses like there was no end to them. I couldn't see any black faces though, and I was looking for them. Some people around me started to cry when they finally got a glimpse of the buses through the crowd. One woman made the sign of the cross and a few others copied her. "I never thought I'd see the day come," said an old woman next to me. She lived downstairs from us, but I had never seen her leave her apartment before. I'd always thought she was crippled or something, sitting there in her window every day, waiting for Bobby, the delivery man who came daily with a package from J. J.'s Liquors. She was trembling now, and so was everyone else. I could feel it myself. It was a feeling of loss, of being beaten down, of humiliation. In minutes, though, it had turned to anger, rage, and hate, just like in those Irish rebel songs I'd heard all my life. Like "The Ballad of James Connolly": "God's curse on you England / You cruel hearted monster / Your deeds they would shame all the devils in Hell." Except we'd changed it to "God's curse on you Garrity."

Smash! A burst of flying glass and all that rage exploded. We'd all been waiting for it, and so had the police in riot gear. It felt like a gunshot, but it was a brick. It went right through a bus window. Then all hell broke loose. I saw a milk crate fly from the other side of the street right for my face. More bricks, sticks, and bottles smashed against the buses, as police pulled out their billy clubs and charged with their riot shields in a line formation through the crowds. Teenagers were chased into the project and beaten to the cement wherever they were caught.

I raced away about a block from the fray, to a spot where everyone was chanting "Here We Go Southie, Here We Go," like a battle cry. That's when I realized we were at war. I started chanting too, at first just moving my lips because I didn't know if a kid's voice would ruin the strong chant. But then I belted it out, just as a few other kids I didn't know joined the chorus. The kids in the crowd all looked at each other as if we were family. *This is great,* I thought. I'd never had such an easy time as this, making friends in Southie. The buses kept passing by, speeding now, and all I could see in the windows were black hands with their middle fingers up at us, still no faces though.

The buses got through the crowd surrounded by the police motorcycles. I saw Frankie running up toward Southie High along with everyone else. "What are you doing out here!" he yelled. "Get your ass home!" He said there was another riot with the cops up at the high school, and off he ran with the others. Not far behind were Kevin and his friends. He shouted the same thing at me: "Get your ass home!" I just wanted to find Ma now and make sure she wasn't beaten or arrested or anything, so I ran home. The project was empty— everyone had followed the buses up the St. Paddy's parade route. Ma wasn't home, but the TV was on, with live coverage of the riots at Southie High. Every channel I turned to showed the same thing. I kept flipping the dial, looking for my family, and catching glimpses of what seemed to be all the people I knew hurling stones or being beaten by the police, or both. *This is big,* I thought. It was scary and thrilling at the same time, and I remembered the day we'd moved into this neighborhood, when Ma said it looked just like Belfast, and that we were in the best place in the world. I kept changing the channels, looking for my family, and I didn't know anymore whether I was scared or thrilled, or if there was any difference between the two anyhow.

* * *

The buses kept rolling, and the hate kept building. It was a losing battle, but we returned to Darius Court every day after school to see if the rage would explode again. Sometimes it did and sometimes it didn't. But the bus route became a meeting place for the neighborhood. Some of my neighbors carried big signs with RESIST or NEVER or my favorite, HELL NO WE WON'T GO. There was always someone in the crowd keeping everyone laughing with wisecracks aimed at the stiff-looking state troopers who lined the bus route, facing the crowds to form a barrier. They never moved or showed any expression. We all wanted to get them to react to something. But we wanted a reaction somewhere between the stiff inhuman stance and the beatings. When my friends and I tried to get through to them by asking questions about their horses and could we pet them, they told us to screw. And it wasn't long before some kids started trying to break the horses' legs with hockey sticks when riots broke out. One day the staties got distracted by a burning effigy of Judge Garrity that came flying off a rooftop in the project. That's when I saw Kevin make his way out of Darius Court to throw a rock at the buses. A trooper chased him, but Kevin was too fast. His photo did end up in the *Boston Globe* the next day, though, his scrawny shirtless body whipping a rock with all his might. It looked like the pictures we'd always seen of kids in war-torn countries throwing petrol bombs at some powerful enemy. But Kevin's rock hit a yellow bus with black kids in it.

I threw a rock once. I had to. You were a pussy if you didn't. I didn't have a good aim, though, and it landed on the street before it even made it to the bus. I stared at my rock and was partly relieved. I didn't really want it to smash a bus window. I only wanted the others to see me throwing it. On that day there were so many rocks flying that you didn't know whose rock landed where, but everyone claimed the ones that did the most damage. Even though I missed, a cop came out of nowhere and treated me just like they treated the kids with good aim. He took me by the neck and threw me to the dirt. I sat there for a few minutes to make sure that everyone had seen that one. I was only eight, but I was part of it all, part of something bigger than I'd ever imagined, part of something that was on the national news every night.

Every day I felt the pride of rebellion. The helicopters above my bedroom window woke me each morning for school, and my friends and I would plan to pass by the TPF on the corners so we could walk around them and give them hateful looks. Ma and the nuns at St. Augustine's told me it was wrong to hate the blacks for any of this. But I had to hate someone, and the police were always fracturing some poor neighbor's skull or taking teenagers over to the beach at night to beat them senseless, so I hated them with all my might. SWAT teams had been called into the neighborhood. I'd always liked the television show "S.W.A.T.," but they were the enemy now. We gave the SWAT sharpshooters standing guard over us on the rooftops the finger; then we'd run. Evenings we had to be off the streets early or else the cops would try to run us down with their motorbikes. No more hanging out on corners in Old Colony. A line of motorbikes straight across the street and sidewalks would appear out of nowhere and force everyone to disappear into hallways and tunnels. One time I had to jump into a bush because they were coming from both ends of the street. I was all cut up, and I really hated them then.

It felt good, the hate I had for the authorities. My whole family hated them, especially Frankie, Kathy, and Kevin, who got the most involved in the riots. I would've loved to throw Molotov cocktails myself, along with some of the adults, but I was only a kid and the cops would probably catch me and beat me at the beach. So I just fantasized about killing them all. They were the enemy, the giant oppressor, like Goliath. And the people of South Boston were like David. Except that David won in the end, and we knew we were going to lose this one. But that made us even more like the Irish, who were always fighting in the songs even if they had to lose and die a glorious death.

One Friday in early October we took part in what Louise Day Hicks called National Boycott Day. Everyone boycotted school again. We'd all heard about the kids who'd gone to school during boycotts and who were threatened over the phone with getting their things cut off. Kevin told Ma we'd better not risk castration, and we got to stay home and watch the rally and march down Broadway. The rally was a good one. When the thousands of people sang the national anthem, with their right hands over their chests, I cried. It was as if we were singing about an America that we wanted but didn't have, especially the part about the land of the free. Louise Day Hicks really squealed that part out from the bandstand microphone, and we all knew what she was getting at.

When the rally was over, the crowds marched to Judge Garrity's home in the Boston suburb of Wellesley. We weren't allowed to go because Ma thought people would surely be arrested. I wanted to go because I'd heard that where the Judge lived everyone was rich and white and I wanted to see what they looked like. But I couldn't, so I just watched the march on its way down Broadway.

The signs at the marches were starting to change. Instead of RESTORE OUR ALIENATED RIGHTS and WELCOME TO MOSCOW AMERICA, more and more now I saw BUS THE NIGGERS BACK TO AFRICA, and one even said KKK. I was confused about that one. The people in my neighborhood were always going on about being Irish, with shamrocks painted on the brick walls and tattooed to their arms. And I had always heard stories from Grandpa about a time when the Ku Klux Klan burned Irish Catholics out of their homes in America. I thought someone should beat up the guy with the KKK sign, but no one seemed to mind that much. I told my friend Danny about the Ku Klux Klan burning out the Irish families, and that the guy with the KKK sign was in the wrong town. He laughed. He said he'd never heard that one before. "Shut up," he said. "They just hate the niggers. What, d'ya wanna be a nigger?" *Jesus no,* I thought to myself.

With National Boycott Day, everything got more scary. In the afternoon, after all the speeches, chants, and the tearful national anthem, crowds gathered at Darius Court once again to taunt the police and to throw rocks at the buses. The TPF chased one man into the Rabbit Inn tavern across the street, and a crowd of people at the bar protected him from the cops. Everyone knew the Rabbit Inn was no place to mess with. That's where the Mullen gang hung out—the toughest bar in Southie. The next night, after dark, we were all called out of our apartments in Old Colony. The mothers on the stoop were yelling up to windows that the TPF was beating people at the Rabbit Inn to get back at them for the night before. Ma wasn't home, so I ran to Darius Court with all of the neighbors, some of them carrying baseball bats, hockey sticks, and big rocks. When I got there, the dark streets were packed with mobs rushing the police. I saw Kevin running through a maze of people carrying a boulder with both hands. He was excited and told me that the TPF had beat the shit out of everyone at the Rabbit Inn, with their police badges covered. Just then I saw people covered in blood being taken from the bar into the converging ambulances.

The mothers in Old Colony showed their Southie loyalty that night. They went up against the entire police force that was filling the streets. I kept getting knocked around by bigger people running in all directions. Someone said the TPF had split open an eleven-year-old's head. I pushed through the crowd to get a look at the kid, and was relieved to see through all the blood that he wasn't Kevin. I wondered if I'd better get home, in case people started getting killed. As the sirens screeched, I saw the blue lights flashing onto the face of Kristin O'Malley, a four-year-old from my building sitting on her big brother's shoulders and smiling at all the excitement. I figured if she could stay out then so could I.

Someone propped up his stereo speakers in a project window, blasting a favorite at the time: "Fight the Power" by the Isley Brothers. We always did that in Old Colony, blare our speakers out of our windows for the whole neighborhood to hear. It was obvious this guy was doing it for good background music to the crashes and thumps of battle.

Everyone sang along to "Fight the Power." The teenagers in Southie still listened only to black music. The sad Irish songs were for the older people, and I never heard anyone listening to rock and roll in Old Colony. One time an outsider walked through Old Colony wearing a dungaree vest with a big red tongue and THE ROLLING

STONES printed on the back. He was from the suburbs and was visiting his cousins in Old Colony. He got a bottle thrown at his head and was called a pussy. Rock and roll was for rich suburban people with long hair and dirty clothes. Mary had a similar tongue painted on her bedroom wall, but that was for Rufus and Chaka Khan; it was okay to like them. Of course no one called it black music—we couldn't see what color anyone was from the radio—but I knew the Isley Brothers were black because I'd seen them on "Soul Train." But that didn't bother anyone in the crowd; what mattered was that the Isley Brothers were singing about everything we were watching in our streets right now, the battle between us and the law: "And when I rolled with the punches I got knocked on the ground / By all this bullshit goin' down."

The mob started pushing and swaying toward the cop cars, blocking them from going down the street. Mrs. Coyne was out there again, and was the first to put a bat through a police windshield. Then everyone surrounded the cops and smashed all of their windows. I started to see things fly through the air: pipes, bricks, bats, and even a hubcap.

Just then I saw my mother pushing through the crowd, yelling at me to run home. "They're beating kids!" she screamed. She kept getting knocked from side to side. She grabbed me by the collar and said she couldn't find Kevin and Kathy; she had a crying voice on her. I didn't want to go home without her, but she made me, while she went looking through the crowds, dodging everything flying through the air. Later on Ma dragged Kevin and Kathy home and gave into us for running up to Darius Court to join the riot. Frankie was still up there, Ma couldn't find him, and we were mad that the three of us couldn't do everything that the older kids could. Ma couldn't yell at us for long; Kevin drowned her out by blasting the television news reports. And soon we were all glued to the set once again, watching for those we knew in the crowd getting dragged into paddy wagons at Darius Court.

On Monday Ma made me, Kevin, and Kathy go back to St. Augustine's. There were no buses coming that day because the NAACP had taken the black students to some kind of meeting at the University of Massachusetts. The black leaders were asking for federal troops to be brought into South Boston, and wanted to see what the black teenagers thought about all that. We didn't want the troops; it was bad enough with the state troopers, SWAT teams, and the TPF, who Ma called "the Gestapo."

We walked to school past Darius Court and up Dorchester Street. The streets were completely empty, still littered with all the things that had flown through the air on Saturday night. Fewer teenagers were finding a reason to go to school anymore, unless they wanted to get in fights. And on this Monday morning everyone had heard on the radio that the buses weren't coming that day, so many in Old Colony stayed home. The silence on Dorchester Street was spooky. I was walking with my head down, looking at all the garbage in the street, when Kevin came up from behind and pushed me. I went flying and when I looked up I saw that I'd been headed straight for a bloody pig's head on top of a post. I let out a yell that should have woken up the neighborhood. I looked up the street, and it looked like something from a horror movie. More signposts with pigs' heads on top of them, some with apples in their mouths. Blood was on the street, scrawled into letters that said KILL THE PIGS or FUCK THE POLICE. We touched the pig's head—we'd never seen real pigs before. I pushed an eyeball and it squished, and then it fell out of the socket onto my shoe. I yelled again. The whole thing seemed more violent than anything I'd seen yet. Whoever had decorated the street with pigs' heads must have been pretty pissed off, I thought, killing some innocent pigs to send a message to the cops.

That afternoon, everyone gathered at Darius Court again, even though there were no buses. The pigs' heads were gone, but you could still see FUCK THE POLICE on the street. The neighborhood was still upset about the TPF beating on women and children at the Rabbit Inn. They were all talking about it when we came upon the crowd. The crowds started chanting again: "Here we go Southie, Here we go!" A circle of teens started rocking a police car that had been left in the middle of the street while the cops chased some kid who'd thrown a boulder at them. They rocked the cruiser from side to side, and just when it rocked high enough they tipped it over on its head. The cops chased them too, but they got away through the maze of tunnels and hallways and ended up on a rooftop at Darius Court, where they threw fistfulls of pebbles onto the heads of their pursuers, who by that time had given up all the chasing and were now inspecting their upside-down cruiser.

I ran further up Dorchester Street when I heard the gunshot. There was a commotion at Jolly Donuts. A cop stood at the intersection with his gun pointed in the air, and he fired a second shot. He was trying to disperse a crowd that was dragging a black man from his car. The man ran from the crowd as people threw rocks at him. More and more angry people ganged up on the black man, who I could see was crying. He was trying to get away, but there was nowhere to go. He ran to a house just outside the project, and tried to climb over a railing. "Kill the nigger!" my neighbor shouted. That was Molly's mother, running to join the commotion. Everyone made fun of Molly at school because they had seen her mother bleeding down the legs of her pants more than once. They said she was so poor she couldn't afford a Kotex pad. But she wasn't as bad off now as the black man, who was clenching his fingers onto the railing of the house before the boys dragged him onto the pavement and beat his skull with baseball bats and hockey sticks. The people living in the house were no help; they booted his fingers off their railing. A photographer flashed his camera at the man from all angles: hands reaching for an escape, baseball bat to the ribs, crying face to the pavement. I remember the man's tears clearing paths in the blood on his face. That's how close I was to him. Scores of police came to the corner at Jolly Donuts and brought out their tear gas and riot shields, and another riot broke out. Kathy and Kevin brought me home and I was sick: sick of the police, sick of busing, sick of being thrilled or scared, and sick of the hate.

The next day it was all over the news. Some pictures were from angles that I could've taken myself if I'd had a camera. Once again I was seeing a replay on the news of what I'd just seen in real life. I was sick of the news too. The newsman said that there were no suspects in the beating that almost killed the man, who was from Haiti and

had been on his way through Southie to pick up his wife at a laundro-
mat. I went back to the site where he was beaten. I don't know why I
was drawn there—maybe I had to feel the sadness, like at a funeral.
I saw an aluminum baseball bat covered in blood and wondered why
the cops hadn't taken it in for evidence, fingerprints and all that.
Whose side are they on, anyway? I thought. They certainly weren't
on our side, and now I knew they probably weren't on the Haitian's
side either.

Ma was mad about the beating, and I was glad about that, because I didn't like being the only one around who wanted to talk
about it. No one else ever mentioned it again. It never happened. "He
probably had no idea what he was driving into," Ma said. She called
him a scapegoat, and I knew exactly what that meant even though
I'd never heard it before. I'd seen it. He was new to this country and
probably didn't even know about South Boston or Old Colony. He
mustn't have known that we all hated the communists, Judge Garrity, the rich liberals, the *Globe,* and the cops, who were all to blame
for the pain in our lives, and he didn't expect that he'd be the only one
my neighbors could get their hands on . . . someone worse off than
us, a nigger.

The day after the Haitian man was beaten, the news said that a white
man driving through Roxbury had been stoned and beaten uncon-
scious by about two hundred black teenagers roaming the streets,
setting fires, and smashing things. They showed the pictures. It
looked like Darius Court, except everyone was black. The news reports made it seem like the blacks were getting back at us. The white
guy wasn't from Southie, though. No way! No one from Southie
would drive through Roxbury; most people I knew had never even
been outside the neighborhood, and since busing no one wanted ever
to leave again. When I was smaller we used to spend hours at the welfare office in Roxbury, with black and white mothers and kids.
Never again!

Nor were we welcome in too many places outside Southie now.
But going downtown once in a while was the only way to get away
from Mayor White's "rule of three," which made it illegal in Southie

for more than two people to stand around on the corners. Kevin and his friends went downtown to scam, so I sometimes followed them. One time they showed me and Danny how to rob the parking meters for bags full of quarters, and we were chased home by a bunch of black kids who knew we were from Southie. We had to run all the way back to the Broadway Bridge, which blacks could never cross over unless they were in a yellow bus. Kevin swore at Danny for wearing his green jogging suit with a shamrock and SOUTHIE on the back. Kevin's friend Okie showed us how he'd covered up the Southie dot on his wrist, the way he always did when he went into town, pulling his sleeves down past his hands.

Ma wanted us to stay away from the troubles. But as much as we tried, it was all around us. You couldn't help being in the middle of it unless you stayed home all the time. And there was nothing to do at home except set traps for the cockroaches. We were getting used to all the craziness from the busing; now on top of it all, it seemed as if the confusion was spilling into people's homes. Teenagers in the neighborhood had started dropping out of school, especially once the police had gained a firm presence at Southie High. State troopers and the TPF were almost in a competition, it seemed, to flex their muscle on our streets. They did their drills in formation up and down Dorchester Street and around the high school. "Hup, two, three, four," with their boots crashing on the road every day before and after school. People still lined the streets to protest, and Louise Day Hicks, Ray Flynn, and Jimmy Kelly kept the rallies going, but the younger people were losing all interest in school. It seemed that all at once, the girls who would've been juniors and seniors were pregnant. And teenagers spent a good part of their day figuring where they could hang out without being caught and arrested for drinking.

Before he dropped out, Frankie was still enjoying the fights at Southie High. He had big fists and a hatred for blacks since he'd been beaten and stabbed on his way to Boston Tech in Roxbury. When he left Tech, he entered Southie High set on revenge. So when-

ever Ma heard the police sirens heading up to the high school, she put
on the TV to get the news flashes that always came on when there was
another riot. She watched, afraid she would see Frankie being arrested for starting another fight. But at least he was going to school,
which was more than many of the other kids in Southie were doing.
One day in December when I was home with the flu, the sirens kept
passing by for a good half hour. Ma turned on the news and heard
that a white South Boston teenager had been critically stabbed at the
high school. They didn't know his name. Ma had a crying voice and
told me to go outside and find out; she knew there'd be more information out on the streets.

There was hardly anyone outside, but those I did see were running up to the high school, carrying things to fight with. At the high
school the streets were so crowded you couldn't move. They were tip-
ping over police cars once again. Just when I'd made it through the
crowd, a woman pulled me back by the arm and I fell onto the pavement. She had saved me from being trampled by a police horse. The
cops on horses were charging at people, the horses climbing on top
of the rioting crowds with their two front legs. I remember looking
at the horses and thinking that they didn't look as if they wanted to
be doing the stunts their masters were forcing on them, knocking
people's heads with their hooves. I found out it wasn't Frankie who
was stabbed, but a kid named Michael Faith.

They'd made all the white kids leave the building. So now the
black kids were in the high school trapped by the thousands of people that I was standing with. I wanted to get home to tell Ma the
news, but now I was stuck. We were surrounded. The police had us
trapped, while we all had the blacks trapped. If I left the safety of the
crowd, I'd be run over by one of the horses or motorcycles that were
surrounding us. And now came the staties, marching in all kinds of
crazy formations. You couldn't tell what direction they would turn
next, and if you were ever in their way, forget it. The only way out
was up, and now that was covered by a helicopter flying in circles
above our heads. It kept coming at us to scare us off, then changing
direction instead of killing us all. Nothing scared this crowd—the

people just gave the helicopter the finger and screamed things into the choppy wind that I couldn't hear. I didn't get home for another two hours, when the riot had simmered down, but all the way home people were still worked up. Teenagers on the corners were doing what they always did at the end of a day of battle: drinking and retelling stories of fights, reenacting blow after blow in slow motion. Michael Faith was in critical condition.

Ma said at this point what's the use in going to school. It certainly wasn't worth the risk of getting killed. Frankie was ready to quit after being kicked out so many times for getting in fights. He'd knocked out one black kid at Southie High and was suspended for ten days. When he'd come back, he'd knocked out another black kid as soon as he walked through the high school doors, and got suspended for twenty days. After twenty days out of school, he'd had no idea what the teacher was going on about at the front of the class. Then yet another racial fight broke out in the classroom, and Frankie'd knocked out one more black kid. That's when they suspended him for thirty days, and Frankie never went back. By the ninth grade he was a dropout, and Ma couldn't afford to send any more kids to Catholic school. I was surprised that Frankie'd ended up a dropout; he was the one who'd always made me sit down after school to recite all of the times tables for him. I knew the times tables before the rest of my class had even started studying them. And besides that, he'd been admitted to Boston Tech in the seventh grade, which meant he was smart, because Tech was an exam school. But that was all before he was stabbed, and long before the buses started to roll.

Mary left school too. She'd recently walked by a black table in English High's cafeteria—black kids sat with blacks, whites with whites—when one of the girls stood in front of her and accused her of trying to have hair like a black girl. Mary had naturally tight curly hair that spread out big and wide on its own. "You wanna look like one of us?!" the black girl said. Mary had already been jumped by a gang of black girls and had had enough. She said back, "What the fuck would I want looking like the ugly bitch that you are?" Then the whole cafeteria erupted into a food fight, which was becoming an everyday occurrence. Mary got jabbed deep with an Afro pick.

She never went back to school after that, and Ma didn't blame her—she just got after her to get enrolled in night school at Southie High. Mary started working full time at Jolly Donuts.

Around the same time, Johnnie was getting his cap and gown ready for graduation from Boston Latin School, and I wondered if this would be one of the few family high school graduations I'd ever see. It was.

NINA REVOYR

Public vs. Private

Several weeks ago, I got into a heated discussion with a usually like-minded friend over whether to send our children to public schools. My friend and I ostensibly want the same things for our children—solid academic instruction, a physically safe environment, access to a variety of extracurricular activities—but we quickly discovered that we were deeply divided on how best to get them. She truly believed that only private schools could provide the things she wanted; I believed that all of those things, and more, could be found in public schools. The argument was somewhat moot, since neither of us actually *has* children yet. But the passions were real.

My friend's reasons for favoring private schools are rational and predictable—she believes they're more academically challenging, less anonymous, and safer; and that they give students "exposure" to all the best in literature, art, and culture. I value those qualities as well, of course, but I have a deep aversion to private schools. They're elitist, I argued, and most of the kids who go to them—or at least to the nonreligious, college preparatory schools—are wealthy, white, and sheltered. And more than I dislike private schools in themselves, I dislike what they represent: the idea that one can pay to be separated from different or "undesirable" people. Besides, how could I work on behalf of low-income kids, advocate for better public education, and get involved in local school board elections—all of which

I do—and then send my own children to private schools? My friend said, "You're sacrificing your children's futures for the sake of your image," and then told me that she didn't want to sacrifice her own children's futures simply to make a political point. This angered me on two counts—first, because I attended public schools and felt that both I and my schools had been insulted; and second, because I truly believe that public schools can do the best job of educating children.

Exactly one week later, I got into another intense discussion about public schools, this one much less theoretical. I was having drinks with a slightly older friend—a single mother who has two teenage sons in a Pasadena public school—when I said that I would never send my children to a particular high school in the Los Angeles Unified School District. Suddenly, I was the recipient of a tirade almost identical to the one I'd unleashed at my other friend the week before. We have to support our public schools, this friend told me, and the best way to improve them is to advocate and agitate while our children are in them. She went on and on about how she was constantly meeting with teachers and counselors and writing letters to administrators, and how parents needed to be more involved in their children's schools. My attitude—that I wouldn't put my children in a public school—was not going to improve the situation. I kept trying to jump in, but she was on a roll, and it was several minutes before I managed to say that I agreed with her; that I'd only been talking about this one particular school, a school that was much worse and more dangerous than the one her sons went to, or the schools that she and I had attended. These two conversations, the first of several I've had over the last few weeks on the issue of public versus private schools, represented the two extremes in the debate over the value of public education. What was striking in all of these discussions was how personally people took them—myself, of course, included. My friends' opinions on public schools, and mine as well, were partly based on fact and partly the result of deeply held views— and biases—on class, race, and opportunity. And all of our opinions seemed to be shaped by our own school experiences, which we either wanted our children to replicate, or avoid.

My experiences in public schools were by no means ideal. When

I first moved to the United States from Japan in 1974, just after my fifth birthday, and started kindergarten in my father's small, backward hometown in Wisconsin, I faced constant bullying and harassment from the other students. Many of the teachers had never taught a child of color before, let alone an immigrant (that my father was from the town and white as a bedsheet got me nowhere), and they were unapologetically racist. And because of their ignorance, their willful blinding to the taunting and physical abuse I received from my classmates; to the special attention I required because of my limited English; I viewed teachers as ineffectual and cowardly, certainly not to be trusted, and school as a dangerous place. Even after we moved to California, when I was nine, and entered a community that was far more diverse, I felt out of place and maladjusted. At some point around junior high school I started acting out. My behavior had consequences, albeit not awful ones: horrid citizenship grades, trips to the principal, detention, at least two teachers telling me I'd never make anything of myself. I attribute none of these difficulties, however, to the fact that I went to public schools; the schools themselves were academically solid. My discomfort and unhappiness had largely to do with my being so different—a feeling that might only have been heightened in a private school.

I actually could have gone to a private high school. Two private schools, both exclusive, academically rigorous schools that sent most of their students to four-year colleges, recruited me to play basketball for them, but after visits to their fluffed-up campuses, I knew I would never survive. I chose instead—to my great fortune—to go to Culver City High School.

Culver High is, in many ways, a typical urban high school. It's large—about sixteen hundred students—old, and in need of renovation. The majority of students are members of racial minorities, and low- to middle-income; and it scores less than the national average on standardized tests. But it was heaven to me, especially after having been in predominantly white schools, both in Wisconsin and then in Hermosa Beach, California. At Culver, I knew kids from Korea, Russia, Mexico, China, El Salvador, Guatemala, Iran, Thailand, Nigeria, Germany, and Denmark. I had several friends whose families had escaped by boat from Vietnam during the war. Over forty languages were spoken at my school, and the student population included, besides the groups I just listed, large numbers of native-born kids of African, Asian, and Mexican descent, as well as Jewish kids. There was even a sizable number of mixed-race kids, and teams and social groups were fairly well integrated. Certainly the school had a few upper-middle-class white kids, but they were such a minority that they had no real power. For the most part, the students were down to earth; there was not a lot of social jockeying or pressure to dress a certain way. No one had much of anything, and so no one showed off; if someone did, that person was seen as pretentious. I felt a social and racial comfort at Culver that I'd never felt before then and have rarely experienced since, and I note the racial and class diversity not to show how *instructive* the environment was, but how accepting. It wasn't that, as a teenager, I thought it would be enlightening to hang out with "those people"—the typical "diversity is good for the mainstream" kind of argument. In fact, I *was* "those people"—an immigrant, a child of color, from a single-parent family; my father didn't make much money and we lived in an area controlled by a gang. And of the six towns I'd lived in by the age of fourteen, it was the one place where I knew I fit in.

The teachers and counselors at my school, for the most part, were patient, tough, and caring; they knew exactly how to respond to my acting out. I'd always done well academically, but I'd also had discipline problems, and by the time I entered high school, the split between my grades and behavior had grown much more dramatic. At fifteen, I was teetering on the edge of several possible futures. I ditched school, disrupted classes, got into open conflicts with two or three teachers. I got sent to the assistant principal's office several times, and was suspended from one class for truancy. But to my tremendous good fortune, I had a school counselor and several teachers who did not let my behavior obscure their knowledge of my ability, and who understood that my problems in school had nothing to do with my intelligence.

But it wasn't just the social and cultural aspects of my school that made me think well of Culver; it was also the quality of the education

I received. I had excellent teachers in every grade, whom I'd put up against any teacher from a private school. Mrs. Goldberg, my first writing teacher, was the first adult I ever really respected. She encouraged my writing and told me what to read; she spent countless hours listening to me, nurturing me, keeping me in line. I learned how to study—and how to love learning—from Dr. Johnson and Mr. Loomer, longtime teachers of history and English, whom my classmates' parents still raved about twenty years after they'd been in their classes. Dr. Johnson could describe the most obscure details of the Hapsburg Empire or the Fourth Amendment and make them sound like the most fascinating facts on earth. And Mr. Loomer, in his stories about famous poets and fiction writers, in his readings of poems, would have whole classes of tattooed, sign-flashing kids staring in rapt amazement. In eleventh grade, Dr. Johnson and Mr. Loomer team-taught the legendary American Civilization class—better known as Civ—a two-hour class that covered both history and literature. And this class, in addition to being the cornerstone of my high school education, also shaped my view of writing—that literature and the world are inextricably linked, and shouldn't be artificially removed from one another, either in study or practice.

Mrs. Goldberg, Dr. Johnson, and Mr. Loomer irrevocably altered my life. They saw through my bravado, didn't put up with my bullshit, and pushed me past what I thought were my own limits. They were completely unimpressed with my accomplishments as an athlete, at a time when my head was huge from the attention I received from the press and college scouts—and the fact that they valued my mind above all else may have been the greatest collective gift that they gave me. They provided me with discipline, structure, and unwavering faith; they gave me an idea of what I could be, and then helped instill the tools to get me there. When I went to college, I was stunned to discover that most of my fellow freshman, the majority of whom had gone to private prep schools, had less knowledge of literature and history than I did.

To be sure, Culver High had problems: there was a gang presence that was usually low-key but sometimes made itself known, and that has grown far more dangerous in the time since I was there. And while the top third of the school did well—and still does—in terms of tests and entrance to college, the majority of the student body does not. But Culver High provided everything I could hope for in a school, and I cannot imagine having been in a more nurturing, structured, accepting, broad, and academically sound environment than I was. And that, quite simply, is more important than having state-of-the-art science equipment and fountains in the courtyard. I know that I am a better person—in terms of schooling, in terms of knowledge, in terms of understanding—for having gone to public schools. To this day, my father apologizes for not having been able to "give me more" when I was growing up, but in never being financially secure, he actually gave me plenty. My peers and I were hungrier, I believe, because nothing was handed to us. Incidentally, Dr. Johnson spent the last few years of his long career at a private school, after forty years at Culver. And he reported that he didn't like the private school students as much—that they didn't seem as ambitious or as interested in learning, and that they took everything they had for granted.

My belief in public education is rooted not only in appreciation for my teachers and peers, but also in a deep suspicion and distrust of private schools. And that suspicion and distrust, I realize, is largely emotional, and is largely based on race and class. I know that many of today's private schools are more racially and economically diverse than they were even fifteen years ago, but their students are still generally whiter and better off than most public school students. In high school, I was acutely aware of these differences in class; they fueled many of Culver City's most bitter rivalries. Beverly Hills High School, for example, was our biggest enemy—the student population there was as exclusive as those in many private schools, and neither the school nor its students were shy about flaunting what they had. The school itself, with it rolling green lawns, lovely buildings, and parking lot full of luxury cars, was as ritzy as an East Coast private college; and the students, many of whom were the children of movie industry moguls or celebrities, were generally obnoxious. Twice when I was in high school, kids from Beverly High vandalized our school; and once, during a football game, the Beverly High cheerleaders came to our side of the stands, and—in a perversion of the standard high school cheer—shouted, "We've got money, yes we do! We've got money, how about you?" My resentment toward Beverly High is so strong that, even today, when I meet people who went there, I go cold for a moment, until I can remind myself that their having attended that hated school doesn't automatically mean that they're evil.

But my classmates and I usually reserved this kind of resentment for private schools. Every time my basketball team traveled to a school where the grass was perfectly clipped and green, where the buildings were beautiful and well maintained, where there were BMWs and Porsches in the parking lots, where the team had expensive sweats and sports bags, where we got stared at when we walked to fast-food restaurants after the game, and where we realized that the fanciness of the school and the team's equipment were reflective of the wealth in the surrounding community—we wanted to beat the crap out of that team, and usually did. Whenever I met a family who could afford to send their children to private school, I considered them to be like beings from a different planet. One of my clearest memories from that period is of crossing paths with my father's boss as I walked to school. He lived in Culver City also, but in the Studio Estates, an enclosed area that is one of the two nicest parts of the city; we lived in an apartment building on a block where the police were daily visitors. Almost every morning, I would see Tim—my father's boss—as he turned out of the Studio Estates, driving his daughter to her fancy private school. And he would wave as I walked to the big public high school that he saw as not good enough for his children.

Eventually, my views of upper- and upper-middle-class people, once totally unsympathetic and oversimplified, became modified and fairer. But I'm still glad I grew up how I did. I liked and respected my peers and their families, who always made so much of so little. And, for better or worse, because *I* didn't want to be surrounded by well-off people when I was younger, I wouldn't want my kids to be, either. The depth of this feeling revealed itself during the argument with my friend, when I yelled at one point with an intensity that surprised even me, "I do *not* want my children going to school with a bunch of rich kids!" This pronouncement came, obviously, from pure class resentment. But I also believe that sheltering kids by keeping them in pretty buildings where everyone has money creates a different kind of ignorance—an ignorance of the world and of people.

When I went to college, the thing that most struck me about the private school kids was how utterly *clueless* they were. They knew nothing about budgeting money, they knew nothing about working, they knew nothing about immigration or poverty or nontraditional families except for what they'd read in books. Despite their good grades and strong academic performance, I thought I'd never been around such a bunch of ignorant fools in my life. As I grew more comfortable in college; as I made friends with some of these kids and realized that I couldn't fairly dismiss them all and that they, too, had real problems and feelings; as I later began to teach—and really care for—the same kinds of kids in a similar college, my anger and resentment subsided. But my opinion of their life smarts didn't change. My friend wants to send her children to private schools for "exposure," but many of the privileged kids I went to school with had been exposed to nothing but the insides of textbooks. Of course, poor kids who'd gone to private schools on scholarships were not so clueless, but many of them had other kinds of conflicts. The wealthy kids knew very little of the world outside of their little rarified circles, and they probably never will. These were young people for whom immigration, poverty, and race were simply abstract principles, not everyday realities. I want my children to be more world-aware than are the private school students I've known. I want my children to see and experience the most important social issues in the country, and not simply study them.

There are, of course, other factors that make both my idealized view of my own public school experience, and the tough and weighted issue of where to educate children, much more complicated than I like to admit. For one thing, as my friend pointed out during the argument, I, even with all of my behavioral problems, was exceptional. It's not only that I did well in school; I was also an athlete, which automatically conferred upon me a certain privilege and status that I would not have had if I had simply been a student. And my problems played out loudly, in public, where everyone could see and respond to them—but what about the quiet, underperforming kid who's overlooked because she doesn't make a fuss? Second, as another friend noted, diversity in a particular school doesn't automatically mean diversity in the classroom. This friend, who's five years older than me, also went to Culver High. But despite her obvious intelligence, academic ability, and talent (she's now a feature writer for the *L.A. Times* and has published a book of essays), she was not placed— most likely because she's black—in advanced placement classes. And I, despite my grades, was never one of the thirty or forty students in my grade who were designated "gifted and talented," thereby making me ineligible for several state-funded programs. Even as I continued to make straight A's, even as I became valedictorian, that distinction never changed.

I also realize that there is a whole slate of good reasons why someone would *want* to send her children to private schools. Recently, I read a quote in the newspaper from a local African-American leader who said that he'd "bought his way out" of the public school situation by sending his son to a fancy private school in Northern California. And who can really blame him? The pressures, dangers, and difficulties faced by young inner-city black and Latino kids—especially boys—are much more complicated and threatening than anything I faced. Even my friend whose sons are in the public school in Pasadena worries that she is endangering them, and perhaps compromising their education, by keeping them in that school. But she's deeply committed to public education, and she wants her sons to go to school with other black kids, so they stay where they are; and she still lives in the same rough neighborhood where she grew up, even though her job and income would easily allow her, if she wanted to, to "buy her way out."

The very real dangers faced by inner-city black and Latino parents were brought home to me this spring when I went precinct-walking in South Central for the school board election. In those humble, high-crime, working-class areas near my office, in neighborhoods where people do not have disposable income, parents are doing everything they can to keep their children out of the local public schools. They send their kids to parochial schools, to magnets and charters, to other private schools. And private schools mean something different for poor families than they do for families who are wealthy. Rich parents send their kids to private schools to hold them apart, but poor parents are trying desperately to *save* their kids, to help them gain access to better lives. If the choice is between sending a child to a dangerous public school where she won't learn anything, or to a private school where she'll feel out of place but be prepared for college, then there really *is* no choice. And this kind of desperation puts a different spin on the school voucher issue for me, because while I oppose school vouchers in principle, the political wrangling over long-term effects on public schools is totally irrelevant to parents who are worried about their children *now*. They can't wait the three or four or ten years it will take to improve public schools. By then it will be too late.

There are plenty of other valid reasons for parents to elect a private school. I have friends who have children with special needs, with learning disabilities, with developmental delays, and it seems logical that they should seek out schools that best meet the needs of their children, and those are likely to be private schools. And all areas are not the same, of course, in terms of school choices. The friend whom I had the original argument with grew up in New York City, where good public schools are much scarcer and harder to access. Even within the horrific behemoth that is L.A. Unified, there are plenty of good individual schools, and there are great schools in the many other local districts. We simply have more options here than my friend does in New York.

I also realize that my argument is not totally consistent because of my own choice of college. With all of my dedication to public education, I attended an exclusive East Coast private university. And while I can say that it never would have occurred to me to go a private college if I hadn't been recruited for basketball, and that the only other school I applied to was a public university—UCLA—it's also true that I jumped at the opportunity. There was simply no way I was going to turn down access to a place like Yale—and I relished the fact that I was accepted there despite my supposedly compromised education in an urban public school. There was a huge "fuck you" factor when I was admitted, which I felt when I saw the adults who'd once told me I wouldn't succeed, which I felt every day my senior spring when I passed my father's boss on the way to school, which my father, who cried when the acceptance letter came, also felt when it was clear his boss was jealous. And which I definitely felt, also, when I was actually *at* Yale, and began to understand that I was no less intelligent or capable than the kids who'd been programmed to go there from the day they were born. I can't explain how I saw choosing a private university as something different from choosing a private high school or elementary school, but I did—and, yes, I'd be thrilled if my kids went to a similar place. Perhaps I saw it as different because all those earlier schools were leading up to something. And college, more than a place to learn, was that "something." It was the ticket to a different kind of future.

I also know that until I have children this is all just an abstract discussion. My children's experiences and needs will be different than mine were. I needed to be around people who were of a similar socioeconomic class, who didn't care how I dressed, who couldn't afford to do much on weekends except play hoops and rent movies, who reflected—or at least accepted—my racial makeup. But what makes my children feel comfortable or accepted may be different. Because of my education and because, even in the nonprofit, social services sector, I already make more money than my father ever did, I have become—much as I hate to admit it—part of a different social class than the one I was growing up in, and so my children will be as well. They will simply *have* more than I did—more material comfort, more access, more supposedly "high" culture, more sense of entitlement—and will probably grow up less angry as well. This, however, doesn't change my conviction that they should go to public schools. I hope to buy a house in the next few months—in itself a marker of my undeniable ascent into the middle class—and when the latest Stanford 9 scores were recently released, I set the scores out side by side with the real estate ads, trying to match neighborhoods that I can afford with good schools. But this activity signifies something else about circumstance and class. I differentiate between a public high school like Culver and public high schools like Locke in Watts, or Belmont in Westlake; and I, unlike many people, have the luxury of *choosing* where to live. I want my kids to go to public schools, but, in all likelihood, I'll be able to pick a community where the public schools are good. If I lived in a place where the only school was not only marginal, but awful, would I want my kids to go there? Probably not. I'd try to send them to a magnet school; I'd try to send them to a charter. But realistically, I might run out of choices.

I want my children to have the best education possible, an education that encompasses life and people lessons as well as book lessons—and I believe that this can be achieved in a public school. I also believe, unlike my New York friend does, that if we're going to advocate and agitate for better public education, we have to choose with our children. We can't just talk a good game and hold our children out of the fray. We cannot abandon our children—and I mean the possessive term here in a larger sense; I mean our *country's* children—in an uncaring, incapable public school environment where they're in physical danger and they don't have access to basic materials. It is our responsibility to the future to try and effect change. But the problem with this picture is that there are two different states of public schools: what they are, and what they could be. If, when I have children, the distance between the two at the neighborhood school is not very great, I will enroll my children there and work with other parents to get it where it should be. But if the distance is so great that it can't be bridged in a year or two, my choice will be much more difficult. My initial gut reaction to the idea of private schools— strong as it is—cannot be the only thing I go on. Would I send my kids to a private school if there were no other viable option? Realistically, yes, I'd have to. But I wouldn't have to like it.

PORTER SHREVE

Neighborhood Watch

Charlie Sackett and I were the only new kids in the seventh grade at Chestnut Hill Episcopal School for Boys, and we stuck out. I was fat, and Charlie had red hair that hovered unpredictably above his narrow face. He wore cowboy boots and a sheriff's badge on the lapel of his blue blazer.

"They let you get away with that?" I asked. By some accident we were assigned the same table at lunch.

"I'm from Texas." He spoke in a *Dukes of Hazzard* accent. "It's part of my heritage."

Later I'd realize that Charlie Sackett had never been to Texas. But he told his lies with total conviction, because in the moment, like all great liars, he must have believed they were true.

At Chestnut Hill Episcopal the lunchroom was a "refectory," the teachers "masters," the swimming pool a "natatorium," and seventh grade was "first form." We had chapel four days a week, prayer before games and meals, and a demerit system that Charlie would avoid but I would not.

Charlie and I were the only scholarship students in the first form —he for his perfect score on the Pennsylvania aptitudes; I because my father, the school's new art teacher, had agreed to supervise the dormitories in exchange for room, board, and a waiver of my tuition.

My family had always lived in Philadelphia, but never this far north, in Chestnut Hill, where the trees grew thick and the neighborhoods raced with children. The school sat on a residential street that was lined on either side with baby mansions made of great blocks of stone and set well off the road, their boxwood-edged walks stretching back to heavy doors. We lived in a two-bedroom apartment at the end of the dormitory hallway. Our cramped quarters were once the chaplain's study, but had been converted when the upper school added thirty dorm rooms for students whose parents lived out of town, out of the country, or, in a few cases, had grown tired of raising children.

My father had never been good at discipline, and before we came to Chestnut Hill, he had never had a reason to be. I was a good kid. I'd been an ace in public school, top of the class. But that was at Horace Mann in Roxborough, where out of boredom, because we had so little homework, I would memorize long sections of *The Guinness Book of World Records* and *The Book of Lists*. At Chestnut Hill, I'd fast discovered, nobody cared about Benny and Billy McCrary, the world's heaviest twins, or the character actor Jan Leighton: the man of two thousand faces, or Kim Ung-Yong of South Korea, who had a two hundred and ten IQ.

Outside the apartment door, kids thundered down the hallways, drilled each other with footballs, shook the walls with Led Zeppelin and Black Sabbath, and smoked pot so nearby that I could smell its sweet dunginess from the sofa in our living room. My father seethed, but did nothing.

My mother, who worked in the school library, would sometimes politely scold them, but they knew well enough that she was out of her jurisdiction.

One day in November, a policeman from the nearest precinct came to assembly to give a talk about crime. He said even the nicest neighborhoods were not necessarily safe, and pointed to a recent rash of vandalism that had happened not far from the school.

"Children have nothing." He paced the stage with a microphone. "They're completely dependent, so at a certain age they start to think, *Enough already; it's time I had my own possessions.*" The officer didn't look like a cop. He had a cop name—Mazzocca—but he was small and wore Buddy Holly glasses.

"Sure, you get an allowance, a nickel here, a dime there. But when you're eleven or twelve, you want to make a life for yourself." Mazzocca stopped behind the lectern, and slid the microphone into its holder. "So you steal. From your dad's dresser, from your mom's wallet, from your own sweet granny." His voice sounded unimpressed, as if to indicate that there was nothing interesting or surprising about theft. "For some it's a phase, a part of growing up. If you're lucky you get caught; we rap you on the knuckles, and you learn your lesson. But if you're not lucky you slip by and keep on slipping until you disappear."

At the end of the officer's speech, I saw my father go up to the stage and take him aside, and that night back in the apartment after yet another refectory meal, my father announced that he had joined the neighborhood watch.

"What do you do?" My mother asked, double-locking the door.

"We drive around and look for anything suspicious. It's a citizen patrol."

My father had begun playing the radio loud after dinner to drown out the noise in the hallways. He played easy listening favorites, so it didn't do much good. I was often teased for his taste in music. During the painting and drawing classes he taught, he set the dial on WBRZ—Easy Breeze, 98.9, and had been known to say, "Let the music lead and your hand will follow."

My father was not the only one in the family making a tough adjustment. Uprooted from her old neighborhood, where she had organized a local reading series and run the vegetable coop, my mother now retreated into the shyness of her girlhood. As for me, I had an A in Spelling at midterm, but failing grades in Grammar, Composition, English, and Religion.

"Ethan's oral deliveries show clear discomfort, the way he mumbles as if not wanting his audience to hear," wrote Paul Bernard, my form master, a gap-toothed Brit with a sleepy eye.

I had tried to do the work. But *Animal Farm* and *Julius Caesar* read like another language to someone schooled only in lists and lit-

tle bits of trivia. I'd sit in the back and with a feigned look of atten-
tiveness count off in my head the twelve greatest villains of modern
cinema, winners of the Cy Young Award since 1957, Harry Houdini's
ten most amazing escapes. I didn't talk back or cause a disruption. I
tried to disappear.

But by and by my classmates began to take note of me. "Look at
Ethan eat. Eatin' Ethan eat." I remember standing in a bathing suit
in front of our bathroom mirror, having signed up for swimming for
the winter term. I had breasts, white slabs of clay for arms. My belly,
black spider legs of new hair crawling across it, hung like a sack over
the tiny trunks they made us wear.

The next day, I dropped swimming for weight training and began a transformation, a personal revolt against the body that had
locked me in.

I maintain that I chose Charlie Sackett, not the other way around.
That first time we met, in the refectory, assigned the same table at
lunch, I asked him about his cowboy outfit, his boots and sheriff's
badge.

"Where in Texas are you from?"

"Near the border," he drawled.

"So you speak Spanish?"

"Sí. Everyone there speaks Spanish." He spooned a second helping of rice onto his plate, poured the creamed chipped beef over it,
and ate as if he hadn't had a bite all day. "My dad worked for Texaco.
We hardly ever saw him, because the men sleep out on the rigs. They
work their shifts by the week, not the day."

Watching Charlie eat, I envied his leanness, his long face. "But
now I see my dad all the time. They moved him to a cushy desk job
in New Jersey."

Charlie had strange, almost yellow eyes that didn't exactly focus
even when he looked at you. He reached across me for a stale roll.

"I miss Texas, and so does my mom. She had to quit her job for
the move. It wasn't easy for her."

"What did she do?" I asked.

"She was, or is, I should say, a zeppelin mechanic."

I had only heard Led Zeppelin—and often at high volume outside of our apartment.

"You know, she worked on blimps," Charlie said.

I looked around to see if we had an audience, expecting another fat joke.

But he continued without a pause. "Nobody in Texas knows more about zeppelins than my mom. Her father, my grandad, was a zeppelin mechanic, too. He worked out of a hangar in Corpus Christi. People say zeppelin travel is dangerous. Ever since the *Hindenburg,* there's been this great fear about it."

Charlie poured himself a glass of milk, then guzzled it down.

"Did you know that the *Hindenburg* could move as slow as five miles an hour or as fast as a hundred? Passengers could look out from the observation deck just as they would on any great ship and see the sights. Imagine taking a zeppelin on safari or down the Mississippi or over the Rocky Mountains. The *Hindenburg* used to take people on cruises over New York City, then park on the needle of the Empire State Building."

"How did they get out?" I asked. The refectory suddenly seemed quiet, as if we were the only ones there.

"Few people know this, but at the top of the Empire State Building, there used to be a 'Zeppelin Room.' The *Hindenburg* would dock and the passengers would take the flight of stairs that wound down through the needle into this great banquet area. And there they'd have a party, looking down on the rest of the world."

Sunlight from the window gleamed off Charlie's badge.

"After the crash, people gave up on zeppelins. They were too dangerous, everyone claimed. But not my grandfather. He designed a new kind of airship that uses not hydrogen, but the nonflammable helium, thousands of small balloons. A simple design that my mother has continued to perfect. My grandfather always said that great inventions are all about timing.

"Do you think we're ready for helium zeppelins?" Charlie Sackett asked.

"We've gone to the moon. I can't see why not."

"Exactly," he said, and stood up to clear his plate.

*   *   *

The next day, lunch assignments changed and I didn't see Charlie Sackett for more than a week. I thought he might have been home sick, but when I asked the lower school secretary, she said she had seen him looking his usual self. After weight training, I went to the public library and checked out three books on airships, and my mother found a microfilm copy of the *Hindenburg*'s original brochure, distributed by Deutsche Zeppelin Reederei, the *Hindenburg*'s founding company.

Everything Charlie had said was true. The whisper-quiet ride, the speed—well more than twice as fast as steamships—the vastness of the great floating vessels, what must have been a revolution in luxury in 1936. "The enjoyment of airship travel makes people sociable, friendships are formed," read a page entitled "A Day on Board." "You finish breakfast and walk to the windows. Down below, you see the long shadow of the airship passing swiftly over the sparkling foam-crested waves of the blue Atlantic, and the joy of experiencing this wonderful achievement in modern travel surges through you."

I read all three books in as many days and asked Mr. Bernard if I could do my next report on zeppelins. I only wished that Charlie Sackett could have been in my same section.

"For a long time you are content to watch the marvelous cloud formations or the effect of the wind on the sea." I stood before the class, enunciating carefully as I quoted from the *Hindenburg* brochure. "And then perhaps you recline on a comfortable chair to read, join a party in a game of bridge, or chat with some new and interesting friends."

I heard giggles from the class but did not look up from my index cards. "The air is delicious and fresh, in fact you seem to have been transported into another and more beautiful world."

When my report was over, Mr. Bernard asked the class if they had any questions. I studied his face for approval, but he sat back in his chair expressionless, arms crossed. After a few moments, where I could actually feel a growing hilarity in the room, a boy in the back raised his hand. His name was Andrew Cunningham, son of the pharmaceutical heir, a classic underachiever who had only country club friends. He had never so much as spoken to me before.

"Why are you so interested in blimps?" he said.

The class exploded into laughter.

I pictured the classroom consumed in flames, Andrew Cunningham falling from the sky. Charlie Sackett and me looking on, as if at an old newsreel, that perfect distance of black and white. And for the first time since my arrival at Chestnut Hill I felt invulnerable.

"To answer your question, I'm not interested in blimps. I'm interested in zeppelins." The muscles in my chest and along my arms trembled. "Blimps have rigid or semirigid frames, making them clumsy, slow and of little practical use. Zeppelins, on the other hand, are fast and as maneuverable as helicopters. Apparently such basic knowledge is not required at the country club."

News of my report reached Charlie Sackett by the afternoon. I was sliding a forty-five-pound weight onto the incline bar.

In gym clothes—a blue-and-white reversible tank top and tight shorts—he seemed skeletal, with jagged shoulders, a concave chest, and the ghostly skin of redheads.

"What are you doing here?"

"Putting myself on your program," he said, and made a scrawny muscle.

The clank of the weights and the whir of the standing fan muted our voices. My boldness of earlier in the day had ebbed. I didn't really want to talk, and Charlie seemed to sense this. Helping him heave up the cold steel of the military bar, his skinny arms straining, I thought about the *Hindenburg,* how in the brochure everything had seemed so hopeful. It could have been describing heaven itself—high in the sky, peaceful and quiet—where nothing can go wrong.

After weight training, Charlie asked me if I wanted to stroll over to the Kit and Caboodle, a package store a few blocks from school where kids went for junk food. I had sworn off the place, hadn't been there in over a month, but I wasn't about to turn Charlie down. He bought a glazed strawberry Pop-Tart and a Welch's grape soda, and I got the same.

On our way back to campus, which at Chestnut Hill they called "the close," Charlie led me down one of the beautiful residential streets. Dusk was giving way to night. The air was still. The neighbors had strung their evergreens in tastefully dim Christmas lights. Red-ribboned wreaths made targets of every door.

"Have you noticed that everyone in this neighborhood has children?"

I nodded in recognition.

"Rich people." Charlie threw his soda can into the street, breaking the silence. "They're breeding."

I watched the can spin around and roll into the tire of a parked car. Ordinarily I would have objected to his littering, in the way I objected to smokers and people who cursed for attention. But Charlie throwing his can somehow seemed right. I crumpled my Pop-Tart wrapper and dropped it on the ground.

"Do you like Chestnut Hill?" he asked.

"The school?" Something about Charlie called for candor. Strange how liars always draw the truth out of you. "I hate it."

He stopped walking. We were standing between two streetlights. His normally pale face in the darkness looked older. The freckles were gone, the boyish hair a mass of intensity now. He seemed more like a man than an adolescent.

"Why?" he asked.

"It's the kids. They're nasty."

Charlie pulled two packets of M&M's from his reversible down coat—navy on the outside, fluorescent orange on the inside—and offered me one of the bags.

I hadn't seen him buy the candy. "Thanks," I said.

"So how are they nasty to you?" he asked.

"They're always on me about my weight, for starters." I stuffed the M&M's into my pocket.

"In Samoa, and many cultures around the world, the more you weigh, the higher your status," Charlie said. "Don't you see this is all about status? You're a scholarship kid, like me. Our geography is different from theirs. At home you're a king. But outside of the kingdom, you're just a traveler." He opened his arms like Jesus. "Look around you. Look at the houses and cars. This isn't your kingdom; it's theirs, and like every empire, they've built it at your expense."

I would have thought this was from a play, that Charlie Sackett memorized lines and then found the right moments to perform them. I watched him with a kind of awe.

"Here." He handed me a pair of wire cutters.

I felt their weight in my palm. Charlie looked up and down the street.

In 1979, all the fancy cars—Cadillacs and Lincolns, Oldsmobiles and Buicks, Jaguars and Mercedeses—had hood ornaments, a throwback to the glory years of the auto age.

I was standing over the long hood of a Lincoln Continental, a silver ship under the shadow of an enormous tree; Charlie was lifting the Lincoln's hood ornament—a cross in a verticle frame. I don't remember his saying anything. I looked at the wire cutters and leaned down and away from the light so I could see what I was doing. Sliding the tool's narrow nose just beneath Charlie's fingers, I thought of the wire as an umbilical cord—it looked like one, the way it wound around.

I squeezed and the cord recoiled like a spring, shooting back into the well of the car. *You're on your own now,* I thought, holding the ornament toward the light. I slipped the cold trophy and the wire cutters into my pocket, glancing quickly around. The living room of the nearest house was dark, the street still silent.

As we approached the entrance to school, I passed Charlie the wire cutters and the stolen ornament.

He handed the ornament back. "It's yours," he said, and walked away.

That night, I searched the apartment for a good place to hide my steal. But the chaplain who used to change his vestments there must not have had any secrets, because I could find no false panels or prohibition closets. I fell asleep with the ornament under my pillow and in the morning stood at my bedroom window holding it out at the extension of my arm, looking through it, as if through crosshairs, at the rich kids filing into school.

As I was standing there, my father knocked on the door. I shoved the trophy into the pocket of my coat.

"Have you seen the front door?" he asked.

My mother was standing behind him, a worried look on her face.

"I should have known that the vandals were right under my nose. Joe said they'd be from the school." The blood had risen in my father's face. Even his eyes seemed flushed.

"Who's Joe?" I asked.

"Joe Mazzocca," my mother said. "He's the policeman in charge of the neighborhood watch."

My mother had a habit of tidying up when she was nervous, which meant our apartment was always clean. She retreated into the living room and started putting things away.

"They've gone too far this time," my father was saying. I followed him out of my room.

On the front door, spray-painted in silver with black outline, was a large airship pointing east, one eye open to the viewer and a long smile across the front. Below the drawing, in large block letters, were the words BLIMP HANGER.

I burst out laughing. I couldn't help myself.

This only made my father more furious. "What's funny?" he asked.

"They spelled *hangar* wrong," I said.

"So you know who did this?"

My mother answered for me. "Ethan gave a report yesterday on zeppelins. It must have had quite an effect on the class." I had never seen my mother's protective side. There'd never been a need for it.

"Well?" my father asked in a way that sounded like accusation.

"I have no idea," I said.

"Rest assured, I'm going to find out." He stormed down the hallway.

Over the next few nights Charlie and I went out several times again, always down a different, equally majestic street. I freed the ornaments from Mercedes sedans, Buick Regals, Chrysler LaBarons,

Cadillac Sevilles, and a couple of cars that might have been vintage, but the darkness made it difficult to tell.

"We won't rest until we've done every car in this neighborhood," Charlie said. He had stopped wearing the sheriff's badge and boots, and he'd had a recent haircut. I figured he was trying to blend in, just as I was with my weight training, so he wouldn't seem suspicious.

"Then what?" I asked.

"What did Robin Hood do?" he said. "How can the good guys win when the bastards have everything?"

Since he neither lived in the dorms nor attended my section, Charlie was one of the few students not questioned by my father about the spray-painting incident. My father refused to paint over the door, doubled his hours on the neighborhood watch, and made regular phone calls from home to check in with Officer Mazzocca at the 28th district precinct. He vowed to the headmaster and the administration, who had become increasingly concerned about the vandalism problem, that he had the situation under control.

My father held one-on-one interviews with students in his small office off the art room that smelled of paint and turpentine. I know, because he interviewed me there.

"Just to be fair," he said, pulling up a hard metal chair for me.

"Where were you during the hours of eleven P.M. and six-thirty A.M. on the night of December 14, 1979?"

"At home asleep, Dad, in the room next to yours."

"Please cooperate, Ethan. You're in the privileged position in this case of being my son, but we do have to go about this methodically."

After a week, my father had yet to find a lead. Officer Mazzocca had called to report an increase in the incidents of vandalism in the neighborhood.

"Why would they want to steal hood ornaments?" my mother asked at dinner one evening.

My father leaned into the refectory table, not wanting the students to hear. "It's classic rebellion," he said. "If it's not the parents, it's me."

"Who says the parents have any right to those cars?" I was quoting Charlie Sackett. "They're parked on the street. The street is public property. Who says they even really own them? Ownership is merely a claim."

I wasn't trying to infuriate my father, but my enemies at Chestnut Hill were so general and numerous that blame for my unhappiness could rest only on him. My father had dragged us to this place, exposed the whole family to ridicule, could not even stand up to teenagers.

"Go to your room!" he said. And I obliged him.

Upstairs, I emptied the hood ornaments from my pockets and laid them one by one on the coffee table in our small living room. I counted twenty-seven pieces, from eleven different makes of car, some even beautiful, worth saving, like the Jaguar that Charlie had helped me pry off an XJ8 and the Mercedes logo that looked almost like a peace symbol. I kissed my first steal—the vertical cross of the Lincoln Continental—placed it in the center of the table, and went to my room to wait.

I imagined that my father had known all along.

"Well?" he said calmly, filling the small frame of my door. He was average-size, but seemed to have acquired a force that made me afraid and strangely proud of him.

Charlie Sackett would say that the ornaments were a plant and point to an open window. "See, that's how the perpetrators got in." He'd pick the pieces off the table and examine them, trying to guess at how anyone could remove them from their mounts. "Amazing." He'd play the innocent and keep the charade alive.

I felt nauseated. My muscles ached. I hadn't eaten a full meal in weeks. I'd dropped eighteen pounds since the start of my program.

"It was me," I said, opening and closing *The Book of Lists,* which sat on the bed beside me.

My father clasped his hands together. "And the door?"

I hadn't thought about the door, but now in my mind's eye I saw Charlie returning to the close late at night after our first escapade, sneaking into the dormitory with his two cans of spray paint, drawing the smiley-faced blimp, intentionally misspelling a word in order to lead the authorities astray. He had done it to acknowledge and protect me. My other classmates didn't have the guts; and what's more I was just a scholarship kid, hardly worth the risk.

"*I* painted the door," I said. It was one of the first lies I had ever told.

My father turned and went back into the living room. I got off the bed and followed him. My mother was sitting on the couch, staring at the floor.

"I'm calling Joe Mazzocca," my father said.

The next day after I returned from weight training, my father took me to the 28th district precinct. Officer Mazzocca, it turned out, was a lieutenant. He had his own office, decorated with trophies and plaques and pictures of Little League baseball teams.

"I coach at the boys' club," he answered when my father asked about one of the larger trophies. "We took the ten-to-twelve championship last year, went nineteen and one."

"Congratulations," my father said.

Mazzocca smiled, sat behind his desk and folded his hands, suddenly serious.

"I understand we've caught a thief," he began.

After a perfunctory lecture, not dissimilar from the one he had given at the assembly, Lieutenant Mazzocca got up from his desk and asked me to put out both hands. I hadn't said a word except "I'm sorry," and "No, I didn't have an accomplice." I thought for a moment that Mazzocca might understand why someone on scholarship would want to even the score with the rich. I knew the boys' clubs in Roxborough; they were full of regular kids like me, whose parents both worked, who got discount bin sneakers from Marshalls, who had never been to Chestnut Hill or even considered the concept of a country club.

The handcuffs pinched my wrists.

"You get one phone call," Mazzocca said.

I looked at my father. His eyes were narrowed; his face betrayed no emotion. I thought of my mother at home obsessively dusting the shelves, straightening magazines on the coffee table, probably crying. Charlie Sackett would be prowling the streets right now with his wire cutters, filling the pockets of his coat. How many cars remained before he could rest? And what would his next project be?

"So?" Mazzocca asked, handing me the phone.

"I don't know anyone," I said.

My father looked at me intensely, hands pressed together, forefingers to his lips. Mazzocca put the phone back in the cradle and took off his glasses, cleaning them with a handkerchief. Outside the window, a squad car pulled out of the lot and flipped on its sirens.

"Well, it's time to take those last steps of freedom." Mazzocca got up from his chair. "You want to do the honors?" He handed my father a ring of keys.

We walked through a large room where policemen were digging into their take-out dinners. The precinct smelled like old newspapers and charred meat. I was grateful that none of the officers seemed to notice us.

The holding cell, on the basement floor, sat at the end of a long hallway of barely furnished offices. It had a bench built into the wall and a sink in the corner and was probably the same dimensions as my room at home.

"Which key is it?" my father asked. None of us had said a word.

Lieutenant Mazzocca pointed to a key that could have been any office key, and my father opened the holding cell door, avoiding my eyes.

I stepped inside, stood behind the bars as my father clanged the door shut.

I gazed at him steadily, but he did not look back.

Mazzocca reached through the bars into the cell and with a small key released my handcuffs. "Good night," he said, and the two men walked down the echoing hallway.

I gripped the bars, the same cold metal of the bench press, incline press, military press, barbells, and listened for their voices.

A door opened, then closed.

The hallway was quiet until morning.

DAVID HAYNES

Make Me

I landed my first teaching gig in the same school district that had "educated" me, the one-high-school working-class Ritenour district in suburban Saint Louis. In hindsight it wouldn't have been my choice to go home and teach, but I have always been a distracted person, and one beautiful May afternoon I looked up and it was the end of my senior year and I realized I had neglected to make plans for the future. My parents showed up with a U-Haul and I went with them.

I had "credentials"* that admitted me to the teaching "profession." I had taken education classes because I always knew deep down that I wanted to be a teacher, though back then I'm sure I would have told you that my interest in this coursework had been purely intellectual. To the extent that was true, Macalester College was the perfect place to nurture my curiosity. Macalester didn't offer a degree in education—I took mine in English—but the college kept in its employ an eclectic gaggle of professors whose job it was to deal with the ragtag misfits among the matriculates of the so-called Harvard of the Midwest who did not intend to continue on into legitimate careers in law or medicine or the running of their fathers' companies.

* There will be a lot of quotation marks in this essay because when you talk about teaching there are a lot of words that are widely used in the "profession" but, which, on closer analysis, don't really mean anything.

The Macalester faculty included Lincoln Ekman, who back then railed against pernicious mathematics and science textbooks and on a regular basis made us go in the lab and actually do exploratory projects. He made us solve equations by moving around brightly colored tiles. Linc would meet with us now and then for the purpose of goading us into telling him what we'd discovered. What many people found was that they really liked textbooks, and while Linc was enough of a sixties guy to allow for dissenting opinions, he made sure, however subtly, that the rest of us recognized how wrong the attitude of the textbooks crowd really was.

Nancy Johansen taught "reading" . . . well, Nancy taught us about books and literature and the magic that happens when those things are mixed with developing minds. The other part—the decoding and the phonics, etc.—she informed us, again subtly, was the stuff of technicians. We'd pick it up. Fast. She was right.

There were other remarkable souls, although at the time I have to tell you I thought these people were absolutely out of their minds, which, in my worldview, wasn't necessarily a bad thing. For language arts we were lectured on Chomsky's work in deep grammar. (Where, I wondered, was diagramming sentences? What happened to the parts of speech? In my indignation I would conveniently forget that I already knew them.) We square-danced, we finger-painted, we played the recorder. Now, a quarter century later as a long-time staff member of the National Board of Professional Teaching Standards, I often hear the best minds in teaching say the same things I heard back then, only affirming them now with decades of research. Who knew?

Arnie Holtz became my personal mentor. He taught philosophy of education, and I took every one of his courses and an independent study or two, as well. Anyone expecting the usual suspects—Aristotle, Aquinas, James, Dewey—would not be disappointed, but Arnie had bigger fish to fry. We read Martin Buber's theological classic *I and Thou.* One of the first articles he distributed concerned the famous Milgrom experiments, where subjects complied when asked to administer shocks to innocent victims. We read Hannah Arendt and Simone Weil, John Hersey's novel *The Child Buyer.*

We'd go to Arnie, some of us, and ask why he had selected these particular readings. Where were the books about the nobility of teaching, the ones that affirmed our genuine goodness and moral superiority at having chosen the humbler path.

A true Socratic, Arnie would ask us why did *we* think he was having us read those books. (Unfortunately the Socratic method is wasted on the vast majority of young adults. We'd answer, "I don't know, why do *you* think we think you're having us read these books?" It would go on like that for semesters.) While at the time I had a few mushy, predigested ideas floating around my (I already told you) distracted brain, I had to teach for a number of years before the real method behind Arnie's madness came clear.

I had never been inside Kratz School, though I'd had close friends from high school who called it their alma mater. One evening in the late sixties, the electricity abruptly went off during *The Man from U.N.C.L.E.* A tornado went over our neighborhood and touched down only briefly enough to rip the ceiling out of one its second-floor classrooms. A decade or so later, room 205 became my home for a year, its accoustical tiles tilted at a slight rakish angle, like those Uncle Bubba fishing hats my father used to wear.

I turned twenty-one on the day that they hired me, the day after Labor Day, just before school started.

"We've got a special setup that I think you'll appreciate," said Bea Hansen, the curriculum supervisor, as she handed me a list of twenty-nine fifth graders. "The ones with the asterisks are in our gifted-and-talented program."

Ten of the names were marked.

"They'll spend most of the day downstairs in special classes. That will leave a much smaller group for you."

That did sound like a deal. She escorted me to the room with the tilted ceiling, showed me where the textbooks were stored and how to find the supply closet.

"I collect lesson plans on Friday, the week before," she said, and wished me luck.

I sat there at the old wooden desk, on a rickety wooden chair.

(One of the untold secrets of schools is that, when a classroom is abandoned for any reason, tribes of scavenger teachers from neighboring villages loot and pillage the forsaken chamber for anything that might be remotely useful, comfortable or functional. That ubiquitous Palmer-method alphabet that borders the chalkboard in front of every classroom in America: someone had stolen my *P*s and *Q*s.)

I had no idea what I was doing—or even where to begin. Room 205 may as well have been the Oval Office or the cockpit of a 747. Like all of my teacher friends, I entered the profession on the fly, as it were. The message seems to be "Look, friend, you spent seventeen years of your life sitting in these tanks. You know the drill. Now get in there and make miracles."

I did the best I could. I made seating charts and planned lessons from the textbooks Bea told me I was required to use. I made one bulletin board for displaying student assignments—I cut out big polka-dot letters that said GOOD WORK! (Bea was a big believer that bulletin boards were a key marker of competence—as if a keen eye for color and facility with scissors and stapler were the portal to pedagogical brilliance.) I had another large bulletin board which I told the kids was *their* space.

"You guys can put anything up here you like," I said.

Happily, most of that first Tuesday and many of the days that followed have faded into the deepest recesses of my brain. I do remember that the students who showed up that day hadn't seemed nearly as impressed at my presence as one would have hoped. Though I can't recall, I'm sure I made some sort of speech announcing my arrival, fresh from the Harvard of the Midwest, returned to my humble roots and bearing the lamp of learning to the likes of them, sweltering in ignorance back here on the home front. I was really glad to be there and hoped we'd have a great year. My reception: cool, blasé, extraordinarily jaded.

Frankly, they couldn't have cared less.

Perhaps that's unfair. Surely, some of them were pleased to see me. I must admit that my recollections are tainted by four really difficult children. Among them, they made that year a living hell.

My fellow fifth grade teachers were not much help. The word *col-laboration* had yet to find its way into the local dictionaries, and the general idea seemed to have been "You're getting paid the same as we are. Get in there and sink or swim." For the record, the pay was $8,800 for the year, which even in the late seventies was not a living wage. My immediate neighbor was a pretty-boy named Larry with a shag haircut, the sort of person who drove a TransAm. He and most of the other teachers treated me with what I have come to believe was a pernicious mixture of classism, racism, and withering condescension. Larry eventually turned into the sort of person one sees in the back of Denny's—jowly, with a beer gut, sitting in a booth with a cocktail waitress he had just picked up at the Miracle Lounge. (This is mean, I know, but people should know better than to treat future novelists as if they were mentally deficient teenagers.)

It didn't further my cause that I refused to frequent the teachers lounge, but I had my reasons. The cooperating teacher with whom I'd student taught in Minneapolis had warned me that such places tended to be hotbeds of gossip and unprofessionalism. "Too many hens—" was the phrase I believe he used. Also there were too many friends of my mother in that room. Coincidentally, my mother provided home day care for several of the teachers in that building. To these women, I was the college boy who played with their daughters in the afternoon, Nikki and Stephanie's big brother. I love these women dearly, but teaching at Kratz School was an awful lot like going to work with one's mother every day. (One day Sandra stopped me in the hall and pointed to a bulge in the calf of my jeans. It turned out to be the previous day's sock. I was twenty-one, raw from the college dorm. This is how we lived.)

My four bad eggs, the problem with this crew: compliance. This is the issue with most problem kids in schools. One kid—I'll call him Steven—was a certified genius who did nothing all day long. Nothing. He was square, like a linebacker, and just as hard to move. Donny and Joe, also not their real names, were classic bad boys, the kinds who pull the cat's tail, throw rotten eggs, and hurl epithets from car windows. "Kenny"'s mother was a raging alcoholic, and the missus was prone to arrive at the classroom door on any given morning, drunk off her ass, and deliver me lectures about the problems with my teaching style.

Suffice it to say, these four did not trot off happily with the gifted crew. They stayed with me every day, and as colleagues will testify, this kind is never sick. Never.

Trouble began right away. The bad boys loved to "nigger"* me under their breath. The alcoholic's kid had a favorite expression: "Make me." "Make me" was his response to almost any request, which in my case was mostly that he please stop making silly noises. He produced spectacular farts through a rather disgusting and agile combination of lips and armpits. Drawing attention to themselves is a kind of specialty for the children of drunks, but I didn't know that at the time.

The genius did nothing. Nothing.† Wouldn't open a book, wouldn't take out a piece of paper, wouldn't pick up a crayon. He sat square in his desk in his spiky brown crew cut, looking at me with a sneer that, like the drunk's kid's, also said "Make me," though the genius was too stubborn to say anything. (I do recall, however, that like the kibitzing uncle we all hate, he had a knack for picking up mistakes I'd make and kept a detailed list in his head, which he'd recite as he passed me on his way into the lunchroom.) In fourth grade he had been subjected to repeated tests that certified his qualifications for the local preadolescent equivalent of Mensa. I remember hearing his IQ and thinking "That can't be possible." I swear to you: he had the highest rating of any person I have ever met or even heard about. That's why the psychologists kept testing him—they couldn't believe it either.

This child did nothing. Absolutely nothing. For nine months.

Early in the semester I went to the principal requesting help. As would be the case in the stifling small world I'd landed in, John Antonio had been my elementary school gym teacher. John always looked

* "Hey, nigger, nigger." "Look what the nigger's got on today." In none of the school districts or individual buildings in which I taught was this behavior deemed worth official punishment. The administrative recommendation: "Ask them nicely not to do that."

† Except go to lunch. It was clear to the naked eye that the genius hadn't missed a meal in a decade.

at my chubby self with the same bemused expression he'd directed to the chubby child version of me a decade earlier, though in principals school they had added to John a veneer of brusque officiousness. We had an employee time clock. Just like at the cookie factory.

"Deal with it" had been John's advice. "Make them do what you want." Not satisfactory advice in my book, though in the interest of full disclosure I remain close-minded to this day to those who thought it a good idea having me run a lap around the playground of Marvin School. So what if the president was passing out fitness medals. I was a delicate child. I have tiny little feet.

I thought about quitting. It was hardly worth the money.*

Bea suggested I try setting up a reward system. As she described the process, I felt the synapses firing, which connected me back to my educational psychology classes. Oh yeah, Skinner, I thought. I know this.

Thus began a career-long sojourn into a shadowy world known as "behavior modification" and its near cousin "motivation." That long ago fall, I discovered that, through a carefully calibrated system of stickers and stamps and concomitant bribes, I could make almost anyone do almost anything I wanted him to do. The bad boys were suckers, cheap dates. They'd bat their eyes sweetly and blush like choir boys for a month on the promise of a Tootsie Roll. The drunk's kid was only slightly tougher. I realized that he was so deep into his mother's disease that, like her, he did whatever he could to get through his day. The one thing he wanted more than anything was the one thing I was unable to give, and that was for someone—anyone, please—to acknowledge how he lived. Maybe I could do that now; I couldn't then. Even so, he relished a hard-earned note to his mother letting her know that he'd only made two farting noises in the past three days.

They were onto me. The whole crew was. I'd learned early on that

---

* General assistance, the terminated welfare program that covered single males, paid almost as much.

rewarding the whole group works best. I'd announce the latest incentive scheme, and they, of course, were all interested in whatever
the reward might be: a Halloween party, a field trip, extra recess. But
the moment I put up the sticker chart, eyes would roll in that way
that only ten-year-old eyes can do. We were hardened cynics, all of
us, even me, though desperate as I was I refused to read their sighs
and bemused faces for what truth they told. I see us now as something like an audience for a lackluster campaign speech, marginally
enthusiastic, none of us believing for a second that taxes will be lowered or the streets will be safer, but willing all the same to accept
whatever patronage might happen to come our way.

Over the years I developed a deep and rich repertoire of motiva-
tional techniques, moving, I tell you with pride, toward more and
more "humane" systems. I would always work in tough, tough
schools with difficult populations.* For me and for the students I
worked with, the choices seemed limited. I could stand in front of
the room and scream myself purple. (Which is abusive and never
works.) I could ignore the disruption and teach those who wanted to
learn and who could manage to hear me over the din. (Unprofes-
sional, unethical, and also ineffective.) Or I could find a way of motivating as many students as possible to join the party. My favorite tool
was a happy-face stamp in a lipsticklike container. It delivered dime-
size blips of motivation to several years' worth of fifth graders in Saint
Paul, Minnesota. It was amazing. I stood at that chart and stamped
away and watched the little shavers pop up in their chairs, with attentive eager looks plastered on their faces. (It didn't seem to matter
much whose names the stamps landed behind.)

More and more I began to get weary. Feel a little sleazy and cra-
ven, like a used car salesman offering free balloons and hot dogs as a
come on. Was every interaction commerce? Didn't anyone do anything for joy, for fun, because it was a good idea, because I said so,
just because?

Of course some of them would, do, did, and I consoled myself

* My choice. Always.

with the fact that my classrooms were for the most part always orderly and my students learned. Still, the doubt continued to burn me.

I should say at this time, that my teacher training had turned me into pretty much a radical constructivist. I believed and still believe that, for the most part, children learn. Period. Our jobs as teachers / mentors / adults / friends is to provide for them rich learning environments, to be experts in content and to understand the structure of knowledge well enough to shape experiences that will allow a learning mind to uncover what is there. I've never been a fan of dumping information in children's brains, though I do believe it is necessary sometimes to do so in order for them to make sense of what they are exploring. I also believe that the basics matter and that this is in no way at odds with having children learn through discovery. I tell you this because it is directly connected to my ultimate disillusion.

Basically, I never had any interest in making anybody do anything. I, myself, had never wanted to be made to do anything. I'm suspicious of an entire system that has predicated itself on the notion that there is a prescribed list of things that must be learned by all and that the job of the teacher is to make them learn it. I believe in mandatory compulsory education, but only to a point. I just don't believe that by definition it ought to have anything to do with what goes on in your basic American public school.

The bottom line: I stopped. I threw away the happy-face stamp (actually, it got stolen: some delinquent is out there in America even as we speak, motivating crack sales with red stamps on an incentive chart). No more posters, no more stickers.

I told my students my philosophy. I told them what my role was and what theirs was and what I believed was available for them to learn.

"I will help you as much as you need. We'll work together. I will not make you do anything. If you don't want to be here, if you don't want to learn, I think that's fine. I just ask that you don't stop others who want to be here from doing so.

"I expect you to control your behavior. If you cannot, here are some places you may remove yourself to until you regain control. It's not my job to tell you when you are out of control. You're old enough to know."

These are the sorts of things I said those last few years I taught in the public schools. For the most part, it worked. Though I got results and consistently had happy students and families, my approach did not buy me any fans among "colleagues" and administration, who believed with all their hearts and souls that my job *was* to make students do X, Y, or Z. At the time my college files remained packed away and I wasn't able to pull together my Arnie Holtz bibliography to tell them why I believed strongly that it was not my job to be a dictator.

I'm not naive. I understand our society as well as most. I work for a living and I get paid—otherwise I would stay home and enjoy the weather. I write because I love to write. I read because I love books.

I genuinely despair of a "what's in it for me" world, where all interactions are mercantile and where people expect credit for enjoying the sunrise. How much of a role did I have in creating such a world? And why wasn't there an alternative to my happy-face stamp? I'd employ it again if I had to: I have no doubts about this. Give me a tough enough class, sure, I'd be up there stamping away if I thought it might be my best bet to get the group in shape, to bring the kids to the point where some real learning could take place. I also do know why Arnie Holtz had us reading Hannah Arendt, why we studied the Milgrom experiment, and I know that every time the ink slaps down on the poster board, my hand will always quaver and I know why that is so.

Back at Kratz, the ship steadied, eventually, though antinausea pills remained a sound investment. The student bulletin board became more or less a running advertisement for the latest Kiss paraphernalia. I spent a year of my life staring at life-sized posters of Gene Simmons and company in full regalia, flaring pink tongues and all. At spring parent-teacher conferences, a Baptist student admonished me in a fit of tears that Kiss was satanic. His parents rubbed his back supportively. I apologized, but the posters remained. It was the kids' space, after all.

My first year teaching wasn't a completely horrible experience. As is true in most classes, the bad apples weren't as many as they seemed at the time—like the squeaky wheels they were, their raucous cacophany continues to live in my memory, while the quieter students retreat to the margins.

Jimmy Brown and his buddies assembled and maintained the Kiss display and showed up on Halloween in full costume, the band's elaborate stage makeup copied to the last detail. Jerry shook my hand to accept my condolences after he returned to school when his mother died, just the way his father taught him, I'm sure. Jan Welman was a frequent contestant—and winner—in juvenile beauty pageants. I could never figure out why. She was so normal and smart and down-to-earth. It bothered me so much I had to write a novel about it to get it out of my system. Theresa gave me a rock turtle which I still keep tucked in the corner of a houseplant. The head fell off years ago.

Becky and Amy struggled so with the basics, writhed with glee at the mastery of a simple computation skill. Shawn Cassidy also set them atremble, though he gained no purchase against the hard rockers who controlled the bulletin board.

Matthew, Dana and Mike and Rod and Steven and Todd and Tina. Tina, who wanted to help. Even when you didn't want Tina to help.

These are their real names, almost all of them, too—and I did not go back to my roll book to refresh my memory. I hope they contact me. I'd like to know what they're up to. Though I get home to Saint Louis now and again, I've run into only one or two over the years. One of the bad boys was in line in front of me at the grocery store a few years ago. He hadn't aged well, in that way that bad boys don't— he was tired-looking and sad around the eyes. He looked stunned, as if life had turned back on him all the things he'd wished on others.

Jimmy rented me a car last year. He looked just the same as back then, except he looked the same age as I do now, and I wondered how that was possible. I forget, I guess, that at the time I knew him he was a little less than ten years younger than I was.

I was not rehired by the Ritenour School District. Something about staff cuts and that sort of thing, and, to be honest, I'm sure they were happy to see the back of me. (For the record, unemployment was a better deal financially: no taxes.) This essay is my thank-you to that first class. Thanks, guys. We survived. We all learned some things. It wasn't so bad, now, was it?

LOIS-ANN YAMANAKA

Obituary

English class, we got Mr. Harvey. Jerome looks at me and puts his middle finger on the desk to our worst teacher, because Mr. Harvey says for the fiftieth time this year:

"No one will want to give you a job. You sound uneducated. You will be looked down upon. You're speaking a low-class form of good Standard English. Continue, and you'll go nowhere in life. Listen, students, I'm telling you the truth like no one else will. Because they don't know how to say it to you. I do. Speak Standard English. DO NOT speak pidgin. You will only be hurting yourselves."

I tell Jerry, "No make f-you finger to Mr. Harvey. We gotta try talk the way he say. No more dis and dat and wuz and cuz 'cause we only hurting ourselfs."

I don't tell anyone, not even Jerry, how ashamed I am of pidgin English. Ashamed of my mother and father, the food we eat, chicken luau with can spinach and tripe stew. The place we live, down the house lots in the Hicks Homes that all look alike except for the angle of the house from the street. The car we drive, my father's brown Land Rover without the back window. The clothes we wear, sometimes we have to wear the same pants in the same week and the same shoes until it breaks. Don't have no choice.

Ashamed of my aunties and uncles at baby luaus, yakudoshis, and mochi pounding parties. "Eh, bradda Larry, bring me one nada

Primo, brah. One cold one fo' real kine. I rey-day, I rey-day, no woray, brah. Uncap that sucka and come home to Uncle Stevie." I love my Uncle Steven, though, and the Cracker Jacks he brings for me every time he visits my mother. One for me and one for my sister, Calhoon. But I'm so shame.

Ashame too of all my cousins, the way they talk and act dumb, like how they like Kikaida Man and "Ho, brah, you seen Kikaida Man kick Rainbow Man's ass in front Hon Sport at the Hilo Shopping Center? Ho, brah, and I betchu Godzilla kick King Kong's ass too. Betchu ten dollas, brah, two fur balls kicking ass in downtown Metropolis, nah, downtown Hilo, brah."

And my grandma. Her whole house smells like mothballs, not just in the closets but in every drawer too. And her pots look a million years old with dents all over. Grandma must know every recipe with mustard cabbage in it. She can quote from the Bible for everything you do in a day. Walks everywhere she goes downtown Kaunakakai, sucks fish eyes and eats the parsley from our plates at Midnight Inn.

And nobody looks or talks like a haole. Or eats like a haole. Nobody says nothing the way Mr. Harvey tells us to practice talking in class.

Sometimes I secretly wish to be haole. That my name could be Betty Smith or Annie Anderson or Debbie Cole, wife of Dennis Cole who lives at 2222 Maple Street with a white station wagon with wood panel on the side, a dog named Spot, a cat named Kitty, and I wear white gloves. Dennis wears a hat to work. There's a coatrack as soon as you open the front door and we all wear our shoes inside the house.

"Now let's all practice our Standard English," Mr. Harvey says. *"You will all stand up and tell me your name, and what you would like to be when you grow up. Please use complete sentences."* Mr. Harvey taps Melvin Spencer on his shoulders. Melvin stands up slowly and pulls a Portagee torture of wedged pants and BVDs out of his ass.

"Ma name is Mal-vin Spenca." Melvin has a very Portagee accent. Before he begins his next sentence, he does nervous things like move his ankles side to side so that his heels slide out of his slippers. He looks at the ceiling and rolls his eyes. "I am, I mean, I wanna. I like. No, try wait. I going be. No, try wait. I will work on my

Gramma Spenca's pig farm when I grow up cuz she said I can drive the slop truck. Tank you."

No one laughs at Melvin. Otherwise he'll catch you on the way home from school and shove your head in the slop drum. Melvin sits down. He blinks his eyes hard a couple of times, then rubs his face with two hands.

Jerry stands up very, very slowly and holds on to the edge of his desk. "My name is Jerome." His voice, weak and shivering, his fingers white. "I in. Okay, wait. I stay in. No, try wait. Okay, try wait. I stay. I stay real nervous." His face changes and he acts as if he has to use the bathroom. He looks out the window to the eucalyptus trees beyond the schoolyard.

Jerry continues, "I am going be one concert piano-ist when I get big. Tank you."

I'm next. Panic hits me like a rock dropped in a hollow oil drum.

Mr. Harvey walks up to my desk, his face red and puffy like a pink marshmallow or a bust-up boxer. He has red hair and always wears white double-knit pants with pastel-colored golf shirts. He walks like Walter Matthau. Mr. Harvey taps my desk with his red pen.

The muscles in my face start twitching and pulling uncontrollably. My eyes begin darting back and forth. And my lips, my lips—

"I'm waiting," Mr. Harvey says.

Jerry looks at me. He smiles weakly, his face twitching and pulling too. He looks at Mr. Harvey, then looks at me as if to say, "Just get it over with."

"Cut the crap," Mr. Harvey spits. *"Stop playing these goddamn plantation games. Now c'mon. We've got our outlines to finish today."* Mr. Harvey's ears get red, his whole face like fire with his red hair and red face.

"My name Lovey. When I grow up pretty soon, I going be what I like be and nobody better say nothing about it or I kill um."

"OH REALLY," he says. *"Not the way you talk. You see, that was terrible. All of you were terrible and we will have to practice and practice our Standard English until we are perfect little Americans. And I'll tell you something, you can all keep your heads on your desks for the rest of the*

year for all I care. You see, you need me more than I need you. And do you know what the worst part is, class? We're not only going to have to work on your usage, but your pronunciations and inflections too. Jee-zus Christ! For the life of me, it'll take us a goddamn lifetime."

"See," Jerry whispers, "now you the one made Mr. Harvey all mad with us. We all going get it from him, stupid."

I want to tell Jerry about being a concert pianist. Yeah, right. Good luck. How will he ever do it? Might as well drive the slop truck if you cannot talk straight or sound good and all the haoles talk circles around you. Might as well blend in like all the locals do.

Mr. Harvey walks past my desk. *"C'mon, Lovey. Start your outline. You too, Jerome."* Sometimes I think that Mr. Harvey doesn't mean to be mean to us. He really wants us to be Americans, like my kotonk cousins from Santa Ana, he'd probably think they talked real straight.

But I can't talk the way he wants me to. I cannot make it sound his way, unless I'm playing pretend-talk-haole. I can make my words straight, that's pretty easy if I concentrate real hard. But the sound, the sound from my mouth, if I let it rip right out the lips, my words will always come out like home.

In our homeroom is Pillis. But Pillis is not her name. Her name is Phyllis. She's the one who pronounces it Pillis. Pillis Pilmoca the Pilipina.

She doesn't look like the midgets I saw on *The Wizard of Oz.* To me, she looks like a regular-looking person except in small portions. Her legs dangle off her chair.

Sometimes I wonder what size clothes Pillis buys. She has this nice sweater with pearl buttons and a chain with hearts across the neckline. Pillis wears it like a cape. If I wear a girl's size 12, I figure she must be a girl's size 6. So small. Sometimes I wish I could have a sweater with a chain like hers.

I hate math, especially fractions. I cannot reduce them, and today I cannot reduce $^8/_{14}$. And no one in the dumbest math class helps me.

Us dumb ones from Mr. Harvey's class go with Miss Mona Saiki for math. And we all like Miss Saiki, except that when math time comes, all the dum-dums have to stand up to leave, while all the smart ones stare and snicker.

If Jerry were in this class, he'd give me the answers real fast. Jerry or Melvin. But I'm in this class with other dum-dums and they laugh at me instead like I'm *very* stupid, stupider than them for not knowing how to reduce a stupid fraction.

"You real stoopid for one fricken Jap," says Thomas Lorenzo. "But you ack real smut when you stay wit' all the odda Japs, eh, girl?"

"Yeah," says Wilma Kahale. "I thought all Japs sappose for be smut. But you cannot even reduce one stupid fraction, eh, you, Jap Crap. Stupid, thass why, you Rice Eye, good-for-nuttin' Pearl Harba bomba."

I feel so small. I want to die. I want to die, it feels like a small little fist inside, twisting.

"What," says Wilma. "What you looking at, hah, Jap? Watch how you make them Jap eyes at me. Like me buss' yo face?"

"Yeah, Wilma. Beef um recess time," Thomas Lorenzo whispers to her.

Die before recess. I put my knees on my chair and draw my body into the desk. I put my head down. I see Pillis from the corner of my eye, thinking very hard.

She puts the eraser part of her pencil in her nose and twirls it around slowly as she thinks. She scratches her head with her short wrinkled finger and writes her answer quickly on her paper. Then she puts the eraser up her nostril again.

"Jap. Jap Crap. Rice Eye. Stupid shit. I catch you recess time, you wait."

They keep talking, so I yell very suddenly, "Ooooh, Pillis, digging your nose with your eraser. Ooooh, Pillis, eraser digger." Thomas, Wilma, and the whole class look at Pillis, so stunned that she leaves the pencil eraser stuck in her nose. Her eyes open wide and buglike.

"Midget digging for small nuggets?"

"Ho, Pillis, stretching your mina-chure nostrils?"

"Midget eraser digging for gold?"

I see Pillis get small, smaller than a girl's size 6, smaller and smaller until she looks like a white-sweatered ball. She shoulder-shakes at her desk and sniffles to Miss Saiki, "I hate them. They make me like die." All of Pillis' pencils and erasers fall to the ground.

Miss Saiki waits. No one helps Pillis. Everyone continues laughing and calling her Eraser Digger. Miss Saiki says, "You are all so appalling. You are dis-gusting." She comes over quickly to Pillis and places her hand on Pillis' back, rubs gently. "Don't say things like that, Phyllis. Everything's gonna be o-kay." Then Miss Mona Saiki tells the rest of us, "Back to work. Now."

Pillis doesn't look at me. She doesn't look at anyone. She smooths her wet binder paper with both tiny hands.

Jerry likes Pillis. So do I, actually. Her big gummy laugh and her short legs that try to kick us when we tease her. She waves to us when the school bus drops her off outside their cane field and her tiny body getting tinier and tinier up the dirt road. She walks eight-tenths of a mile to her house next to the sugar mill.

I don't know what to say. Jerry would know. But I don't tell him.

That night, I struggle with my math problems on the linoleum table. My mother asks if I need my father's help. I tell her no, I'm just reducing fractions. The light above the table slides across the binder paper.

I think about Pillis. I put my pencil eraser up my nose. What a wonderful feeling, especially when you twirl it and you have to think. I do this to the other nostril too.

My mother tells me to knock it off. To get a Kleenex instead. I wonder if Thomas Lorenzo and Wilma Kahale are at home trying Pillis' eraser digger too.

I don't know what I'll say to Pillis tomorrow. I don't know if she will ever wave at me from outside the school bus again. But I know now how she feels. It is something I have always known.

Here lies Jerry all cold and skinny. He was a good son. He tried very hard to learn how to swim.

C−.

Here lies Lovey dead as a doorknob. She hated math and shot a mongoose.

D−/F.

We had to do this twice already. Every time we study a newspaper unit, we end up making a newspaper in class. The smartest girl be the editor-in-chief, the most creative one be the features editor, the boy best in dodgeball be the sports editor. Lori Shigemura be the "Dear Lori" column so she can read all the problems, try solve them, and then tell the whole world who "I Honestly Love You, Junior Ah Chong" or "Stone in Love with Raymond" really is.

And this newspaper is not even typewritten. And the rest of us beat reporters write articles about "The New Turtle in Rm. 5." Or "Fifth Grade Dances to the Age of Aquarius."

Then you know it, we gotta write our own obituary. Like I even care. Dead is dead. Can't see or feel or care. I seen dead. Dead rabbits. Dead dogs. Dead goats. Dead sheep. Dead chickens. Dead fish. You name it, my father shown it to me.

I saw my Aunty Kawa dead. They made her wear peach lipstick and a nice satin peach dress. Like somebody should've told them she wore red lipstick every day and a plaid button-down shirt with denim knickers.

And all of her family, they kissed her dead face, even my mother—but when my mother lifted the veil for me, I couldn't do it. Her face looked like stone.

Jerry says it's fun to write our own obituary. Like witnessing our own funeral. He wants to see all the people he hates and who hate him attend his funeral to cry. Of course, he wants me to play songs like "Seasons in the Sun," "Wishing You Were Here," "You've Got a Friend," and "I Haven't Got Time for the Pain" so that the people cry more.

Me, I don't want to go deaf or blind before I die of old age, but if I had to choose, I'd rather be deaf and learn sign language than blind and have to buy a Seeing Eye dog.

Please God forbid that I go crazy before I die.

And God forbid that I die by drowning and have that frantic, leg-kicking feeling I had when Jerry's big brother, Larry, held my ankles down in Mizuno Pond or suffocate with a pillow or garbage bag over my face with my claustrophobia.

I think about dying every night. Sometimes I want to die at strange moments in the day. Sometimes every day. My mother says it's all those books I read about concentration camps. The arsenic in the heart that I tell her about and the gas chambers with fingernail markings on the walls and ceilings.

Once I thought about suicide. Maybe twice or three times. Once when Clayton Young, who had the longest bangs with side comb for a skinny second saxophone player, said I smelled like his sister's rags to the whole woodwinds section. Twice when Jamielyn Trevino, the butchie in ceramics, pulled the chair out from under me, then whipped a wad of clay across the room which splat flat to my forehead. Three times when I heard my uncle say to my aunty in the kitchen that "Cal and Lovey, yeah, maybe my sista Verva right when she brag that they cute and well behave, but they stupid, stupid, stupid." I was sitting in his garage. He thought I'd walked home. I wanted to dedicate my death to them with a suicide note that said, "Lovey, yeah, maybe cute, but stupid, stupid, stupid."

Grandma said to me a long time ago that the Bible says suicide is a sin. Those who do it burn in the eternal flames of hell forever and will never see Jesus' sweet face. Grandma says when I die of natural causes, I'll be with Jesus, and she tries to describe the warm light and eternal peace, but it sounds like a long, hot nap to me.

Sometimes when my grandma leaves for Moloka'i, I feel like a funeral. It's a big hollow ache inside of me. Even if we did have to eat fish-head soup for two nights, then mustard cabbage and pork soup the night before she left.

I lie very still at night and wonder when I'll see her again and why days go by so fast when she's here.

This year, Mr. Harvey says, *"What would you do if your parents died in a train crash?"*

Jerry says, "Ain't no trains in Hawai'i." But he puts his head down to think.

Mr. Harvey makes us close our eyes and tells us about the changing landscape, the awful crash, the blood, the body parts, the glass cuts, and the screaming, all while we see it in our minds.

This is what I *want* to write:

If my parents died in a train crash, God forbid, knock three times, I'll probably live with my grandma on Moloka'i, who makes me take Flintstones vitamins every morning and eat S & S saimin with chopped green onions, scrambled eggs, and sliced Spam for lunch.

At five o'clock Aunty Bing will drive the Malibu to the drugstore where Grandma works. Grandma will have a whole box of chocolate wafer candy in gold paper for me.

One weekend, we'll go to Vacation Bible School. I make miniature gospels with matchbooks and construction paper. We write a Bible newspaper based on the stories by the apostles like we were there to interview them and call it *The New Testament Tribune*. I write a headline called "Jesus Born in Bethlehem Manger."

I'll advertise in the classified ads. "Wanted: A New Bible. Not the King James Version." And maybe Grandma will put one on my bed for me. Then we'll carve Ivory soaps into crosses or Virgin Marys.

At night, Grandma will cut watermelons and Aunty Bing and me sit on the porch and eat watermelon and sunflower seeds and spit the seeds and shells on the driveway.

All of this I'll do over and over again until Pal, Grandma's poi dog, comes home from the gully after two heats with her new litters of puppies.

This is what I actually write:

If my parents die in a train crash. I dunno what I am going do.

D−/F.

Jerry writes:

If my parents die in a train crash. Then stops. I see him thinking. I know he's about to take this too seriously, and when he does, he might cry.

"I dunno what I might do if my parents dies. Who going buy all the food and bath soap and where I going eat at night?"

Mr. Harvey listens to our whispering and lets us go.

"What if I all by myself, Lovey," he says, "can I live with you?"

"You and me can live with my grandma on Moloka'i," I tell him, "and pick pineapples for Del Monte and go to church on Sundays with Grandma and clean the communion glasses and eat the leftover communion crackers. You and me," I tell him.

I don't want him to cry. He starts to write his obituary. All the things I told him we would do.

Here lies Lovey.

When she died, she didn't know how or why. She did not attend her own funeral like she planned. What do angels look like, so she'll know when she gets there? And Grandma, if you get there first, don't yell "Lovey, Lovey," because I might be deaf, or wave your arms, because I might be blind.

Lovey is dead. Come close when you take me home. I know you by the smell of a brand-new Bible and green onions on your fingers. I know you by the feel of gold paper.

JEFF RICHARDS

LD

I flunked first grade. Or rather I was afraid of first grade. Or my teacher, Miss Cave. I remember what she looked like. She looked dark. Every morning after milk and cookies, she shoved us into a big, dark room and closed the door. We were supposed to fall asleep on threadbare cots covered in army blankets, which would have been fine if I could have seen my hand in front of my face, much less the toy soldiers I brought along to play with. It was too dark, darker than midnight. I begged my grandmother to let me return to kindergarten. She was my substitute mom while my other one was in Warm Springs, Georgia, with my older sister who had polio. My grandma was a skinny little woman with a big head covered in orange hair, a chicken neck, and ropy arms. Her eyes seemed twice the normal size behind the thick lenses of her glasses. She liked to clean the dirt lines on my neck, the cracks behind my nose. She stuck a washcloth in my ear and twisted. She marched into the bathroom unannounced while I sat in the bathtub naked. She was almost as scary as Miss Cave. But she consulted my father and they went to the principal at John Eaton Elementary School and soon I was back in kindergarten with Mrs. Myers, a sweet, gentle lady with gray hair styled in a poodle cut who reminded me of Mamie Eisenhower.

This is why I flunked first grade—this fear—or at least that's the

excuse I've given until I found out I was born LD. I must have con-
tracted it in the womb or maybe I caught it from the dirty laundry.
Most likely it came in my genes because my mother and daughter are
also LD, though only my daughter, Hannah, has been diagnosed as
such. I remember that Hannah's diagnosis was a revelation, of sorts.
Now I knew that it was not Miss Cave's dark room but her classroom
I feared the most. I felt liberated that I could name the true source of
my fear but, at the same time, I felt confined by the name. Learning
Disabled. Especially disabled. This suggests that there is something
missing or, at least, doddering about my brain. But we're not doddering; our brains are just wired differently. Other people, that is,
the vast majority of Homo sapiens on earth, make connections in a
logical, linear fashion, $1 + 1 = 2$. In our minds, $1 - 5 + 3 - 20 + 22 +
1 = 2$. We arrive at the same conclusions but it takes us a while longer
to get there and we travel over some interesting terrain on the way.

Our minds are twisted but they are perfectly good minds. We are
artistic, sensitive, impulsive, socially and emotionally immature.
Spaced. We are angry, passive, withdrawn or overly extroverted. We
tell stories in random order without references, and our academic
skills are very slow in developing. At least that's the way we are when
we are young, according to Neela Seldin, a specialist in LD who com-
piled the above list of our characteristics. When we grow older, we
either adapt or don't adapt. Some of us drop out of high school and
clerk at Kmart. Some of us graduate with Ph.D.s in nuclear physics
and work for NASA. Some of us are well known: Harry Belafonte,
Cher, Vince Vaughn; or leaders in their fields: Dr. Donald Coffey, a
cancer researcher at John Hopkins; Dr. Florence Haseltine, a pioneer in women's health issues; Gaston Caperton, the educator and
former governor of West Virginia; and Roger W. Wilkins, the civil
rights activist. According to the Learning Disabilities Association of
America, I'm also in the company of Winston Churchill, Thomas
Edison, Albert Einstein, Leonardo da Vinci, all of them either LD or
afflicted by one of LD's numerous cousins, like dyslexia. Da Vinci
often wrote from right to left. He had difficulty completing projects,
leaving scores of complex plans and designs for posterity to try to as-

semble. Ms. Seldin describes the young disabled student as one who "can't make choices" and "can't stay with an activity." "Distractible, impulsive." The type to sketch out and set aside.

Those of us with Learning Disabilities, in other words, occupy every rung on the ladder and apparently always have, which leads me to wonder what all the fuss is about. Speaking from my own experience and that of Hannah and my mom, I have to believe that the discovery of LD as an actual psychological disorder is as much the result of social change as it is of scientific study.

My mom was home schooled until she was twelve. Then she attended the public schools in her small town in Ohio, graduated from college, and worked for five years until she married my dad. All this with a defective brain at a time when working women, much less those with educations, were frowned upon. I don't know what kind of struggle her parents went through to educate her but it must have equaled my own, because my mom and I are cut from the same cloth. We are both blue-eyed, the same light blue with darker blue facets like marbles that I can see as well in my daughter's eyes. When I look in Hannah's eyes I see my mother, a spooky feeling at first, though in the end comforting, as though I am raising my mother who raised me. More comforting still, strangely enough, is that we all have the same twisted brain.

Take, for instance, how the Learning Disabled "tell stories in random order without references." We used to say that Mom reminded us of Faulkner. She'd tell us about a brooch she saw at Lord & Taylor, then she'd switch to a dream she remembered from last night about how I was a doctor who was about to operate on her and before we could figure out the Jungian significance of this, she'd switch to her plans for dinner and how she'd seen a child cross the street against the light on Wisconsin Avenue, ran out to stop him, and almost got hit by a car.

"You never know when your time is up," she'd say. "So you might as well enjoy life while you can."

And on and on she'd go. One story piled on top of another until our heads were spinning, and then she'd turn her hand over to show us the brooch. "I decided to buy it," she exclaimed. "Isn't it beautiful?"

I'm not at all like my mother in this way. I don't tell stories. I keep them to myself. They bounce around inside my brain like Ping-Pong balls. Even the most trivial event turns into a story in my head. My daughter, Hannah, sits in the backseat of the car telling stories to herself usually about animals while I drive her to school. Breeze, our parakeet, or Fluff, our bichon, are the heroes. Often her stories are layered and complex. Breeze meets a cockatoo. Fluff saves Breeze from the clutches of Fred, the tom across the street. There's no end to the detail.

I don't know exactly where our twisted narratives began, though I suspect with my mother's mother. I have a photograph of my grandparents when they were teenagers. My granddad's eyes are flinty, focused, while hers are big, round, spaced-out eyes. They seem to be turned inward. If I look closely I can see they are faceted and, I guess, even though I can't tell since it is a black-and-white photo, her eyes must be blue. I imagine that she inherited her disability from her father, Captain Steward of the 101st Ohio Volunteers, veteran of I don't know how many Civil War battles, if any. He could've been in ordinance. But, if I let my mind go a little, I can picture a bivouac on the Tennessee River 130 years ago where an officer leans back in his camp chair before a huge campfire piling one story on top of another as his comrades look on in amusement.

I can imagine that, or further back, a millennium, to one of my blue-eyed disabled ancestors holding a sword to King John's neck yelling, "What? What?" (we also have difficulty hearing) while King John yells back, "I'll sign, I'll sign."

It is a nice feeling to know that in our labile emotions, our anger and excessive silliness, with our focus on what is happening inside our heads rather than in front of our blue eyes that we have managed not to step off a cliff or impale ourselves on a sword, that we have managed to survive in spite of Darwin's laws or, should I say, because of.

There is certainly one positive about our disability: Hannah and

I enjoy rich inner lives. My wife, on the other hand, has to be on the phone or working all the time, always on the move. My son is the same way. Rollerblading, baseball, television, anything so long as he doesn't have to sit still or entertain himself. Hannah and I can take or leave the external world, which is a danger, I suppose, because if we leave it, we could easily become hermits. Or, as an apparent indicator of LD suggests, we'll become "socially off-base." So tag us out.

But if we all agree that imagination and creativity are essential to human survival and, since those of us with this disability have an overabundance of said quality, then counting us out might not be such a good idea. A short list of things made possible by imagination: planes, trains, automobiles, haiku, the wheel, refrigerators, rubber bands, the atomic bomb. I don't want to discount logic. The theory of relativity is, after all, mathematics. But when I said the existence of Learning Disabilities is as much a result of social change as it is of scientific study I neglected to note that I have this fear, perhaps unreasonable, that those in authority—the nebulous "they"—want to do to us what nature could not. They already tried with my mom and now they're going to work on Hannah. They moved her out of the classroom to a special school. They want to regroove her brain so it's not twisted anymore. They tell us that she can come back when she fits in better, when she doesn't mishear anymore, when she's totally focused on group activities. When she is the *same*. When she is *normal* as defined by the extremely narrow parameters of normal that seem to be going around these days.

In my day, things were different, just as they were in Mom's. We were normal though we were dense, lacking in gray matter. Stupid. That was okay for Mom, perhaps. It was the job of women in her era to appear inferior to men. How else could they catch a husband? But for a "provider" in the making like myself, it was a disaster. That's why I was afraid of Miss Cave. It wasn't the Freudian implications, but rather the fear of being found out. That's why with the help of scary Grandma, I sought out the relative safety of Mrs. Myers's kindergarten. Mrs. Myers, like Mamie and dear, old grandfatherly Ike. Howdy Doody. Hopalong Cassidy. Pancho. Jingles. Ozzie and Harriet. All those warm, fuzzy characters from the fifties who kept me away from the nasty realities of the world. Mrs. Myers read stories to me. She let me scribble and finger-paint and build blocks in the corner and play quietly with my neighborhood friends who were all in the same grade, though a year younger than I. It was a comfy feeling even though sometimes on my way home from school, Newt, the neighborhood bully, pushed me down in the bushes and knelt on my face. He thought this was funny. In my dreams, I still smell his sweaty fists.

By the time I moved on to first grade to the benign Miss Gibbs, who did not shove us into a dark room and close the door, I developed a strategy. It was not difficult considering that Miss Gibbs also had to deal with Newt, and Pete, the class clown who broke everyone up with his imitation of an old man and a young man farting. Or Tommy, the teacher's pet, who hung on Miss Gibbs's every word. His mom had recently died and I could tell she felt horrible for him. Or the thirty-odd other personalities that were allowed in the classroom because the parameters of normal were much wider back then. My strategy was easy to pull off in the midst of the confusion—hide out in the back of class behind the tallest kid. I didn't say a word, but gave the impression of working diligently at whatever task was at hand. When the teacher came by, I hid the pictures of warships or airplanes I had been drawing. I knew if she found out she'd think I was screwing off, or worse, that I couldn't do the work, that I was a fraud, a fifth columnist or a pinko infiltrating an educational institution. This was the fifties.

I followed this strategy throughout my career at John Eaton Elementary and I thought it had been a great success. But as my fourth grade report card, an artifact from that bygone era, indicates, I wasn't fooling anyone. In it, I received zero checks in Outstanding Progress, four in Satisfactory Progress in areas mostly to do with deportment, and sixteen in Needs Much Improvement, the lowest grade, in academic subjects. This remained consistent for the whole year until the last period when I received fourteen in Satisfactory Progress and was passed on to the fifth grade. Shame on you, Miss Probey. She must have been overwhelmed, like Miss Gibbs who had passed me on to the second grade, and so on and so on until the sixth, when it came time for me to graduate and the principal pulled my parents aside to inform them that I was not to move on to Alice Deal Junior High with my buddies, but to Bell Vocational, where I would prepare for a career in the industrial arts. I could be an air-conditioning specialist, a car mechanic, a truck driver. I'm not denigrating these professions. I'd get a kick out of truck driving and the pay's not bad, especially, I hear, if you own your own rig. But what if I had wanted to be a lawyer, God forbid? In those days, I wouldn't have stood a chance. They believed in the assembly line, the tract system where you were either college prep, high school grad, or me.

Was I really that stupid? Was I unable to calculate fractions or percentages? Or understand what I read? I enjoyed comic books. *Fantastic Four. Archie. Spiderman.* Even the high-brow Classic Comics. One of my fondest memories was going to the drugstore to buy those comics with my dad, who seemed to enjoy them as much as I did even though he wasn't LD. I hated *Dick and Jane.* Who didn't? But comics aside, I have to admit now, I could not read worth a damn. I was no whiz at fractions. And besides the baseball statistics I computed and recorded in a spiral notebook, I knew little of percentages. Though the terminology didn't exist at the time, I was LD.

My parents were upset at my failure to move to the next level but were undaunted, as concerned parents tend to be. They arranged for me to be tested at a diagnostic center. They enrolled me in summer school and endless tutoring sessions, and transferred me to Longfellow School for Boys where I repeated sixth grade. I remember I was very depressed. I wanted to run away, join the circus or the merchant marine. I didn't want to leave my neighborhood buddies to go to this bizarre school in Bethesda full of boys who dressed up in blue blazers and ties everyday.

The summer before I went to this school, they gave us a reading list—*Penrod* and *Tom Sawyer,* the usual collection of coming-of-age classics. I remember sitting in the bedroom of our rented beach house feeling the sticky, salt air, looking up occasionally from where I was bent over a book to see the yellow curtains blowing in the window. I'd hear the far-off waves against the shore, the wind in the pines, and I'd feel like I'd just woken up from a long sleep. I could read. I could *really* read. And later on, after I had finished another book, I would sit down at my desk and write exhaustive synopses and commentaries.

I hated my parents when they enrolled me at Longfellow but, when I went there and my new teacher read an excerpt from one of my book reports and said I had some good ideas, I accepted the possibility that they might be onto something. My teacher could understand my writing; I could understand him and follow his instructions; I passed tests and did my homework without copying from the encyclopedia. For the first time in my life, I didn't feel like a fraud.

However, I wasn't instantly cured of LD. It is a disability and not a disease. My mind is still twisted and always will be. What is different is that I learned how to deal with it. I'm easily distracted, so when I was in a college class I concentrated by taking elaborate notes. Many students borrowed my notes since I missed almost nothing of what the professor said. I think they benefited more than I did given my problems with memory. So I tested poorly. I made up for this in out-of-class assignments where I had time enough to think about what I was going to say. On these papers, teachers would act surprised and wonder if I was the same person who wrote the exams. My professors did not understand that I had a twisted mind, that I was as smart as anyone else, that I came to the same logical conclusions as everyone but it took me longer to get there because I was distracted by the interesting terrain I traveled on the way.

Today my daughter's teachers know what mine did not. This is both good and bad. It is good that they've found the terminology. The Internet has hundreds of Web sites that relate to Learning Disability, some of which define LD with as many as forty-eight different characteristics. Hannah has only a handful of these, many of them similar to mine: "academic skills very slow in developing, strong discrepancies in skills and knowledge, artistic, sensitive, excellent vocabulary but poor production, wants to tell but cannot retrieve words, mishears or doesn't hear, and problems with various motor development–related skills." I am amazed, on the one hand, by what a good job the nebulous "they" have done in codifying my disorder, but, on the other, I am frightened by what they plan to do

with all this ammunition. They are, after all, tinkering with the human mind, my daughter's mind, in particular, and I don't find this
reassuring.

I believe they are at the very beginning of understanding LD, but
don't yet know how to treat it. Or if it is treatable. Or if it is a disability. Or a difference, which is closer to my view. When Hannah was
in first grade she received a report card much like my own from Miss
Probey. Only Miss Probey was a nice lady, even nicer when she
turned into Mrs. Bernard in the middle of the year. Hannah's teacher
was a prison guard. She looked like Miss Honey in *Matilda,* but
acted more like Miss Trunchbull so let's call her Ms. Honeybull.
Ms. Honeybull's range of normal was ludicrous. Only about three
students could fit into it, two of whom were on Ritalin, the third
naturally passive. She was always berating the students for one thing
or another and keeping them in from recess for minor slipups such
as talking out of turn in class or not keeping in line when the students walked from one classroom to another. Once, she even beat
one of the students with a ruler for not identifying the location of the
Nile river on a map. One of Ms. Honeybull's favorite victims was
Hannah.

Hannah with her pretty, round Irish face like her mother's, thin
lips, and long hair to her shoulders, flyaway hair like mine. She's been
a vegetarian since she was five. She hates that we own a leather couch
though she does grudgingly sit on it. When her skin touches the
leather, sometimes she'll say, "This is disgusting," and eyeball us half
in jest as if we are murderers.

When we received Ms. Honeybull's report card, we were upset
that Hannah flunked absolutely everything. We knew she was having difficulty in her academic subjects but we had received no prior
warning that it was this bad, even in art which she loves. How could
she flunk art or, even more inexplicably, deportment? We were aghast
with the accusations that she didn't show consideration and respect
for others, that she didn't play or listen to her peers, or cooperate or
share, or control herself, and on and on. This was antithetical to
every experience we had ever had with our daughter. Only a kid who
burned down the school deserved grades like this, said my wife. We

arranged a conference with Ms. Honeybull. She defended her views. We defended ours. Nothing much was accomplished. As we left the conference room, Ms. Honeybull blurted out, "Your daughter is unteachable."

"Now I understand," I might have said but didn't. It wasn't that Hannah was unteachable. It was that Ms. Honeybull was incapable of teaching Hannah. Connie, my wife, thought it went beyond that. "They're trying to push her out of the school." Which seems obvious to me now as I look back on it. We did what my parents did when we were growing up. We tested Hannah. We hired a tutor. We looked for other schools.

By the fall of the next year Hannah was enrolled in the Lab School of Washington, one of the premier schools in the world for children and adults with learning disabilities. Unlike Ms. Honeybull, the teachers are trained to deal with a wide range of students, using art, theater, dance, woodworking, hands-on experiential methods to teach academic skills. For instance, in order to build a cabinet in woodworking, you must know math. Sally Smith, the founder and director of LSW, is the recognized leader in the field of learning disabilities. In addition, she is the head of the graduate program in LD at American University, author of five books on the subject and countless articles. As tough a character as you're likely to find, she could squeeze blood out of a turnip. So the school is well endowed. But not exclusive. Most of the students are funded and come from the public schools. The waiting list to get in is endless, as is the waiting list for teachers who want to teach there. But the real judge of LSW's success is that 90 percent of the students go on to college.

Hannah is thriving in this environment. She is much further along in her reading, writing, and arithmetic than I was at her age. She is happy. The teachers never punish her. They never single her out, except for praise. They have given her the award for good behavior practically every week she has been there. If she accumulates enough of these awards over a certain period of time, she is allowed to have lunch with the handsome gym instructor that all the girls swoon over.

In the fall the Lab School gives a gala at which they honor success-ful people with LD. I think it was the year they invited the Fonz that a paleontologist from Johns Hopkins, Dr. Steven M. Stanley, said in his speech to the overflow audience at the Omni-Shoreham Hotel that he thought he wasn't disabled. I don't remember his words ex-actly but they confirmed my belief. His brain, like my own, was twisted. It took him through that same illogical Alice in Wonder-land world that I go through daily, and when he came out on the other side, usually he came out with a scatter-brained idea. But sometimes when he came out, his ideas were great, the very same ideas, he thought, that made it possible for him to rise to the top of his field. His twisted brain was no disability. It was a gift.

What Hannah has, what I have, what my mom had, and what our ancestors had back to the guy who held the sword to King John's throat—were gifts. And yet, I'm still apprehensive for Hannah. Will she be at the Lab School forever? Or will they recommend a transfer to a more traditional school once she catches up developmentally with her peers? Either way, I wonder how well she will do in college and beyond. Will she be able to compete in the real world? My con-cerns are no doubt little different from other parents'. Yet other par-ents do not have to go to the expense, the extra time, and the heart-ache that Connie and I do. Somehow I feel cheated that we are forced to send Hannah to a special school with kids who are basically the same as she. I wonder why this is so, why she must be isolated from the average student population, the $1 + 1 = 2$ crowd.

We seem to be in a contradictory period in American education. On the one hand, we preach diversity and multiculturalism. We want our children to be exposed to as many different types of people as possible. On the other hand, we are practicing a new kind of segre-gation. All races are, on the surface anyway, welcome in our schools so long as everyone acts normal. But the range of normal today is less broad than it used to be. It does not include those with LD. It is in-creasingly exclusive.

Take Newt, the neighborhood bully. He eventually stopped as-saulting people, graduated from college, and now runs a successful company and serves on the board of the Special Olympics. Pete, the class cutup, is a travel agent, who has been all over the world with his English wife. Or my sister and her best buddy, Howie, who went to Quaker school. They loved to pull pranks such as dropping marbles on the floor during Quaker meeting or shooting off cap guns. My parents were forever receiving notes home from my sister's teachers about her atrocious behavior. Now she is a university professor, author of over forty books. Poor Howie was Special Adviser to the President of the United States.

I mention these successful adults because if they were around today as elementary school students they would likely be diagnosed with Attention Deficit–Hyperactivity Disorder, ADHD. In today's schools, these kids would be given various doses of Ritalin, a drug that supposedly helps you concentrate, though it only masks who you are until it wears off and you crash in the same way you used to crash on LSD in the sixties. What a bummer. I wonder which is better, the old way where Newt was allowed to work out his problems with the help of his parents, teachers, and friends, or the new way, where the drug does the lion's share of the work.

These are two ways to prevent diversity—drug the kids in the classroom and kick them out. In my time, the teachers said, "Boys will be boys." But now boys are not allowed to work out what is naturally inside them. One proponent of the belief that boys are in trouble suggested that the Littleton massacre might have been caused by boys who were forced to conform this way. I wouldn't go that far, but I do understand the essence of his point. If you can't work out aggression in one way, it's going to come out in another.

There is something repellent about nature, if I judge certain educators correctly. Those who are hyperactive or have natural aggression should be drugged. Those of us born with twisted brains should go somewhere else until we fit into the classroom again. Perhaps I'm paranoid, but I think we might be headed for a future where certain people will be assigned to the scrap heap as a way of preserving the purity of the classroom. Isn't this a kind of social engineering that should sound alarms? Something that can never work because it is founded on ignorance and a prejudice toward what is *different*?

ASHLEY WARLICK

What We Come Across

I have never been a conscientious student, a doer of homework, a studier. I believe in the nugget of knowledge, the detail that makes what you haven't experienced yourself familiar, and I think you can make it through the world just fine if you have that one detail about everything. It makes for a different focus, doesn't it?

As I recall, it's not an outlook particularly encouraged in the school system, but who can blame them for that? It eventually becomes impossible to quantify one person's knowledge in relationship to a bunch of peers. That's a good thing. That's why we don't go to school for our entire lives.

But we do keep learning. I keep a list of things I didn't learn in school, the oh Jesus commonsense things that might seem obvious enough to pass unsaid. At some point in my life, I have found these things to be profound for their simplicity, or, at the least, neat to think about. I write them down for my daughter.

1. Memory begins when the fontanel closes.
2. The slaves buried their dead at night, because they had to work all day.
3. When you drive past a meadow of cows, they are all female.

I wonder how her life will be different, knowing these things in advance of figuring them out for herself, or reading them in a book when she is thirty, or having to pretend at a cocktail party, that yes, of course, she knew that. I believe the time at which we come to understand something does change us. The people who lay out school curricula believe that too. There is a time when we are most open to understand cursive lettering, trigonometry, Chaucer, and because we grasp these concepts, we can move on to other, bigger ones in a great big developmental chain of events. Early on, my daughter will trust her memory. She will consider the constraints of work, the nature of where we get the things we use. What will she think of next?

In my first nursery school class, there were five children, three of whom were named Ashley. That says something significant to me I have yet to figure out. Once I went to kindergarten, I spent thirteen years at the same school, which means I had the time and the exposure to pretty much figure that place out, and for those people to feel they had me pinned down too. When my first novel was published, my best friend ran into our high school English teacher in a bookstore. He is a marvelously strange man, a man who believed as much in King Lear as he did transcendental meditation. He taught us all how to throw the I Ching, and we were not the kind of students who might have picked something like that up at home.

When my best friend saw him in that bookstore, he had stopped teaching at our old school. Our class had been one of his last. They spoke of my novel. He said he had seen my potential for that kind of work way back when I'd been seventeen. He characterized it as an emotional maturity, akin to something sexual, something, he said, you could sense coming off me. This, too, I have yet to figure out. It is ever hard to see yourself in context.

I don't have fond memories of high school. But it was in this man's English class I first experienced the way something can happen that makes me think I sense more than I know, and it's that thinking I've come to rely on as a writer.

It was Sunday of Memorial Day weekend, the weekend before I was to graduate high school. My father and I planned to drive my grandmother to Casar, North Carolina, to visit her own mother's grave. It is a great tradition of my grandmother's family, and maybe of her generation, that Memorial Day is spent remembering those that are no longer with us, spent most often in church, or in cemeteries. She was no longer able to drive herself, and so we were going to take her to her home place, her family church, then her sister's house for lunch.

I had just finished writing a paper on Eudora Welty's use of birds in *The Optimist's Daughter*. I remember I'd chosen the book because I'd never read anything of Welty's, and I am the daughter of an optimist myself. But it was the light, constant presence of birds that caught my attention; I was taken with the puzzle of symbolism at that age. There was a flock of starlings Laurel fixed on at her father's funeral, the mockingbirds that attended the gossip of the neighbor ladies in her mother's garden. She remembered, with distaste, the pigeons that ate from each other's craws when she visited her mother's home place in West Virginia. None of these birds were peace doves, no clean images of freedom or flight, and I appreciated that.

At any rate, it was the final scenes that got me; Laurel spent her last night alone in Mount Salus sealing herself off from a chimney swift trapped in her parents' house. I had never before come across the superstition about a bird in the house foretelling a death in the family, or the idea that it's swallows that carry our souls to heaven. I will be forever charmed by superstition, but even with that charm, it was a tense stretch of pages. Laurel could hear the bird beating itself against the walls of the house all night long, and it was clear she did not like birds. It was clear this bird gave her the willies.

The house my grandparents lived in was not the house my father grew up in. This house was large and brick. It had been built when I was an infant, in a clearing of scheppernongs, at the end of a long asphalt drive lined with magnolia trees, behind a circular fountain my father had helped my grandfather lay the stone for. Neither man was a mason; I can never remember seeing the fountain work, and it might be true that the thing never worked at all. It was hard to remember the heydays of this place on that morning in May. The crabgrass was high. The dogs were all dead, or gone. It would be one of the last times I'd see my grandparents in this house, their own home.

It took a half hour to convince my grandmother to come with us.

Her protest was mostly back and forth, dithering from the kitchen sink to the kitchen counter to the sink again. She said how she was busy. She had to make supper for John T., but yesterday's supper was still on the stove. It didn't matter; she just didn't have time to go with us. My father said how her sister was waiting, and she gave him a look. She said, you know not, which was something she said a lot to my father. But then something else was set in motion, and there was much looking for her purse, for things she wanted to make sure she carried with her wherever she went. At that time, she carried quite a bit in her purse—deeds to properties, Bible leaflets, a bottle of Oil of Olay. I have memory of my father nearly dragging her to the car.

There were still the roses to cut for the grave. The same rock that made the fountain in front of the house had underlaid most of the land before it was farmed. What boulders of it had been blasted up, some hired man bulldozed into three great piles around the cleared lawn. My grandmother had planted these piles with blaze red roses, climbers. We had never been allowed to play in the rocks as kids, because they were full of snakes, but now my father was climbing all over them, to cut the goddamn roses, to get on the goddamn way.

He was losing his temper. He is not a man with an especially fast temper, as men go, but in those days with my grandmother, it did not take much. I understood, even then, how it was not her he was angry with, how it was hard to have your mother's mind go feeble, and how it made him angry in that way that you get angry about unfairness and lost chances and things you cannot help. Too, she was incontinent. This made her restless, distracting in her ever-motion and possibility for mess. She did not like to stand still or sit still, and would not be still in the car, and so he was already losing his temper in preparation for what was to come. It was hard for him to ask his mother if she'd wet herself, and I could understand that too.

She was losing her mind, and my grandfather was dying from emphysema. By the fall they would check into separate nursing homes and my father's oldest brother would sell their house from underneath them, so they would have to stay. But that Sunday, the fall seemed far off. It was hot, the way it can be hot in May in North Carolina, and gray-skied, near to rain. We were driving a Chrysler convertible, with the top up, twining the back roads from York County to Casar. I was driving, because my father was needed with my grandmother in the backseat, where she still felt we ought to turn around and take her home.

The road to Casar is the road through the foothills, Kings Mountain and Shelby, Cleveland County. There were truck stops and car dealerships and then just miles and miles of greening land, some pastured, some planted, and then more truck stops. It was not familiar highway to me, but it had a place in familiarity. I had known my great-grandmother before she died, could remember visiting her in Casar, could taste a dustiness in the back of my throat that called to mind this countryside. There was part of me sealed off from the backseat of the car and the high emotion there; there was part of me enjoying the drive.

The car was a metallic burgundy color, the color of pomegranates.

From the side of the highway, a bird rose up. I hit it with the car. I'd never hit an animal with a car before, and I felt the impact of that small thing against my travel forward. The sound was heavy and solid. My hands became tight at the wheel.

Then there was another bird. Miles later, another after that.

I don't know how many birds I hit in all, but I know it was enough to vanish the possibility of coincidence. It was like driving through a hail of birds. I began to think, if I rolled down the windows, the birds would fly into the car itself, and what would that mean? I was convinced this had to mean something, and here's why.

I kept thinking of the bird in Welty's house. I kept thinking of the way birds could be dirty and dumb, the heavy dust of death in that book. I was driving my demented grandmother and her favorite son back into their past, and passing through something out of the Bible or Hitchcock to do it. I felt weight and portent. I felt alone, like if I were to speak, no one would have known what I was talking about. And so there is this question—would I have noticed these birds had I not been noticing birds in *The Optimist's Daughter*?

I think so, but I don't think I would have held this day as long in my memory, or as highly. Something from school informed something that happened in my life, made an event seem heavy and strange with fate and purpose, and how intoxicating is that?

It is strange to recount this story now, ten years later. The context has changed yet again. Now, my grandmother is dying, and soon I will drive with my family to see her in a hospital room for the last time. I know this. It does not seem like a bad thing to know.

I will have occasion to ask my father if that fountain in front of their house ever worked, and he will tell me it did, and that one fall he and the hired man dyed the water in it purple for the Grape Festival. I will ask him if he remembers that Memorial Day and he will tell me he does, and how he thought the birds must have been drawn to the color of the car. I will be surprised on both counts, but then feel that I have remembered something significant, something important and worth remembering. And then, when the time comes, we will make that same drive, to that same cemetery.

But for months, I have been thinking of that day with the birds on the road to Casar, and in the process of writing this essay, I have reread *The Optimist's Daughter* twice. The book, the thinking, the event of that trip and the event of now all seem linked to me, delicately, loosely, the small way life strings things together when you pay attention. It was there, then, with that book and that drive, that I learned how it can happen when you pay attention. It was there I first saw what I keep looking for now, as a writer. When a book takes something common and layers it with just the right amount of history and time and insight, it makes magic. It makes people out of words on paper, people as familiar as family, people you call on when you need them. I have the idea it's wanting that familiarity that keeps me at my computer long after everybody else just wishes I'd come make dinner.

Recently, I was in Mexico City during student demonstrations. Thousands of students, college students, impossibly young people marching on the *zócalo* in an effort to effect their rights. They felt they should be allowed free schooling, indefinitely, which sounds outrageous, but it is actually the way things have been for years. Mexico is in the process of trying to privatize the university system, two hundred and fifty thousand students strong at UNAM alone, and it is talking tuition increases, time limits, other uncomfortable things like that.

It was a cause important enough for the students to take to the streets. They carried banners and gave off chants. They marched down Avenida Madero to the *zócalo,* and, as they emptied into the enormous square, a boy, a young man lay a U.S. flag at their feet.

A few stepped over it, some on it, some ground and wiped their feet. Someone found a can of spray paint and sprayed a swastika over the field of stars.

It was my first experience with this kind of thing; I am myself too young for the flag burning of the 1960s. I felt confused, somewhat guilty. Were they angry at the U.S. because our university system was in better straits? I am still paying off my undergraduate loans, will be into the next decade. But with the swastika, that didn't seem to be the point, did it?

I got to thinking about what happens when we put symbols in the hands of those who are too young to value them. Maybe those people aren't so much looking for what something means, as they are looking for the effect that meaning has on others. Effect seems easier. Effect is the tangible thing, the water in your face, the cheese behind the right door. Effect, for me, some years ago, was the smack of birds against my car, and let me tell you, that was startling. Uncomfortable. But, *why?* That has to be the question.

I got to thinking it was time for these students to be heading back to school.

I was watching all this from the high terrace of my hotel, over the square, and I was glad to be out of the way of the people who thought so poorly of my country, when across it all, from the far side of the pavement to the near, came a new bride. Her gown was full and white, its hem lifted from the street, and her hair was swept up and pinned with flowers. She was flanked by men in tuxedos, women in chiffon, a child. She did not rush. She did not seem frightened by the demonstrators, merely passing through them, and they did not seem to notice her at all.

And maybe that's why I am more interested in the dumb, commonsense things these days, the things that don't need much teaching to be learned. I will remember that bride in white, her grace, her lifted hem, long after I've stopped wondering what the stars and stripes have to do with Nazis.

CHARLES BAXTER

Gryphon

On Wednesday afternoon, between the geography lesson on an-
cient Egypt's hand-operated irrigation system and an art project
that involved drawing a model city next to a mountain, our fourth-
grade teacher, Mr. Hibler, developed a cough. This cough began
with a series of muffled throat clearings and progressed to propulsive
noises contained within Mr. Hibler's closed mouth. "Listen to him,"
Carol Peterson whispered to me. "He's gonna blow up." Mr. Hibler's
laughter—dazed and infrequent—sounded a bit like his cough, but
as we worked on our model cities we would look up, thinking he was
enjoying a joke, and see Mr. Hibler's face turning red, his cheeks
puffed out. This was not laughter. Twice he bent over, and his loose
tie, like a plumb line, hung down straight from his neck as he exploded himself into a Kleenex. He would excuse himself, then go on
coughing. "I'll bet you a dime," Carol Peterson whispered, "we get a
substitute tomorrow."

Carol sat at the desk in front of mine and was a bad person—
when she thought no one was looking she would blow her nose on
notebook paper, then crumble it up and throw it into the waste-
basket—but at times of crisis she spoke the truth. I knew I'd lose
the dime.

"No deal," I said.

When Mr. Hibler stood us up in formation at the door just prior to the final bell, he was almost incapable of speech. "I'm sorry, boys and girls," he said. "I seem to be coming down with something."

"I hope you feel better tomorrow, Mr. Hibler," Bobby Kryzanow-icz, the faultless brown-noser said, and I heard Carol Peterson's evil giggle. Then Mr. Hibler opened the door and we walked out to the buses, a clique of us starting noisily to hawk and cough as soon as we thought we were a few feet beyond Mr. Hibler's earshot.

Five Oaks being a rural community, and in Michigan, the supply of substitute teachers was limited to the town's unemployed community college graduates, a pool of about four mothers. These ladies fluttered, provided easeful class days, and nervously covered material we had mastered weeks earlier. Therefore it was a surprise when a woman we had never seen came into the class the next day, carrying a purple purse, a checkerboard lunchbox, and a few books. She put the books on one side of Mr. Hibler's desk and the lunchbox on the other, next to the Voice of Music phonograph. Three of us in the back of the room were playing with Heever, the chameleon that lived in the terrarium and on one of the plastic drapes, when she walked in.

She clapped her hands at us. "Little boys," she said, "why are you bent over together like that?" She didn't wait for us to answer. "Are you tormenting an animal? Put it back. Please sit down at your desks. I want no cabals this time of the day." We just stared at her. "Boys," she repeated, "I asked you to sit down."

I put the chameleon in his terrarium and felt my way to my desk, never taking my eyes off the woman. With white and green chalk, she had started to draw a tree on the left side of the blackboard. She didn't look usual. Furthermore, her tree was outsized, disproportion-ate, for some reason.

"This room needs a tree," she said, with one line drawing the suggestion of a leaf. "A large, leafy, shady, deciduous . . . oak."

Her fine, light hair had been done up in what I would learn years later was called a chignon, and she wore gold-rimmed glasses whose lenses seemed to have the faintest blue tint. Harold Knardahl, who sat across from me, whispered "Mars," and I nodded slowly, savoring the imminent weirdness of the day. The substitute drew another branch with an extravagant arm gesture, then turned around and said, "Good morning. I don't believe I said good morning to all you yet."

Facing us, she was no special age—an adult is an adult—but her face had two prominent lines, descending vertically from the sides of her mouth to her chin. I knew where I had seen those lines before: *Pinocchio.* They were marionette lines. "You may stare at me," she said to us, as a few more kids from the last bus came into the room, their eyes fixed on her, "for a few more seconds, until the bell rings. Then I will permit no more staring. Looking I will permit. Staring, no. It is impolite to stare, and a sign of bad breeding. You cannot make a social effort while staring."

Harold Knardahl did not glance at me, or nudge, but I heard him whisper "Mars" again, trying to get more mileage out of his single joke with the kids who had just come in.

When everyone was seated, the substitute teacher finished her tree, put down her chalk fastidiously on the phonograph, brushed her hands, and faced us. "Good morning," she said. "I am Miss Ferenczi, your teacher for the day. I am fairly new to your community, and I don't believe any of you know me. I will therefore start by telling you a story about myself."

While we settled back, she launched into her tale. She said her grandfather had been a Hungarian prince; her mother had been born in some place called Flanders, had been a pianist, and had played concerts for people Miss Ferenczi referred to as "crowned heads." She gave us a knowing look. "Grieg," she said, "the Norwegian master, wrote a concerto for piano that was," she paused, "my mother's triumph at her debut concert in London." Her eyes searched the ceiling. Our eyes followed. Nothing up there but ceiling tile. "For reasons that I shall not go into, my family's fortunes took us to Detroit, then north to dreadful Saginaw, and now here I am in Five Oaks, as your substitute teacher, for today, Thursday, October the eleventh. I believe it will be a good day: All the forecasts coincide. We shall start with your reading lesson. Take out your reading book. I believe it is called *Broad Horizons,* or something along those lines."

Jeannie Vermeesch raised her hand. Miss Ferenczi nodded at her.

"Mr. Hibler always starts the day with the Pledge of Allegiance," Jeannie whined.

"Oh, does he? In that case," Miss Ferenczi said, "you must know it *very* well by now, and we certainly need not spend our time on it. No, no allegiance pledging on the premises today, by my reckoning. Not with so much sunlight coming into the room. A pledge does not suit my mood." She glanced at her watch. "Time *is* flying. Take out *Broad Horizons.*"

She disappointed us by giving us an ordinary lesson, complete with vocabulary word drills, comprehension questions, and recitation. She didn't seem to care for the material, however. She sighed every few minutes and rubbed her glasses with a frilly perfumed handkerchief that she withdrew, magician style, from her left sleeve.

After reading we moved on to arithmetic. It was my favorite time of the morning, when the lazy autumn sunlight dazzled its way through ribbons of clouds past the windows on the east side of the classroom, and crept across the linoleum floor. On the playground the first group of children, the kindergartners, were running on the quack grass just beyond the monkey bars. We were doing multiplication tables. Miss Ferenczi had made John Wazny stand up at his desk in the front row. He was supposed to go through the tables of six. From where I was sitting, I could smell the Vitalis soaked into John's plastered hair. He was doing fine until he came to six times eleven and six times twelve. "Six times eleven," he said, "is sixty-eight. Six times twelve is . . ." He put his fingers to his head, quickly and secretly sniffed his fingertips, and said, "seventy-two." Then he sat down.

"Fine," Miss Ferenczi said. "Well now. That was very good."

"Miss Ferenczi!" One of the Eddy twins was waving her hand desperately in the air. "Miss Ferenczi! Miss Ferenczi!"

"Yes?"

"John said that six times eleven is sixty-eight and you said he was right!"

"*Did* I?" She gazed at the class with a jolly look breaking across her marionette's face. "Did I say that? Well, what *is* six times eleven?"

"It's sixty-six!"

She nodded. "Yes. So it is. But, and I know some people will not entirely agree with me, at some times it is sixty-eight."

"When? When is it sixty-eight?"

We were all waiting.

"In higher mathematics, which you children do not yet understand, six times eleven can be considered to be sixty-eight." She laughed through her nose. "In higher mathematics numbers are . . . more fluid. The only thing a number does is contain a certain amount of something. Think of water. A cup is not the only way to measure a certain amount of water, is it?" We were staring, shaking our heads. "You could use saucepans or thimbles. In either case, the water *would be the same*. Perhaps," she started again, "it would be better for you to think that six times eleven is sixty-eight only when I am in the room."

"Why is it sixty-eight," Mark Poole asked, "when you're in the room?"

"Because it's more interesting that way," she said, smiling very rapidly behind her blue-tinted glasses. "Besides, I'm your substitute teacher, am I not?" We all nodded. "Well, then, think of six times eleven equals sixty-eight as a substitute fact."

"A substitute fact?"

"Yes." Then she looked at us carefully. "Do you think," she asked, "that anyone is going to be hurt by a substitute fact?"

We looked back at her.

"Will the plants on the windowsill be hurt?" We glanced at them. There were sensitive plants thriving in a green plastic tray, and several wilted ferns in small clay pots. "Your dogs and cats, or your moms and dads?" She waited. "So," she concluded, "what's the problem?"

"But it's wrong," Janice Weber said, "isn't it?"

"What's your name, young lady?"

"Janice Weber."

"And you think it's wrong, Janice?"

"I was just asking."

"Well, all right. You were just asking. I think we've spent enough time on this matter by now, don't you, class? You are free to think what you like. When your teacher, Mr. Hibler, returns, six times eleven will be sixty-six again, you can rest assured. And it will be that for the rest of your lives in Five Oaks. Too bad, eh?" She raised her eyebrows and glinted herself at us. "But for now, it wasn't. So much for that. Let us go to your assigned problems for today, as painstakingly outlined, I see, in Mr. Hibler's lesson plan. Take out a sheet of paper and write your names in the upper left-hand corner."

For the next half hour we did the rest of our arithmetic problems. We handed them in and went on to spelling, my worst subject. Spelling always came before lunch. We were taking spelling dictation and looking at the clock. "Thorough," Miss Ferenczi said. "Boundary." She walked in the aisles between the desks, holding the spelling book open and looking down at our papers. "Balcony." I clutched my pencil. Somehow, the way she said those words, they seemed foreign, Hungarian, mis-voweled and mis-consonanted. I stared down at what I had spelled. *Balconie.* I turned my pencil upside down and erased my mistake. *Balconey.* That looked better, but still incorrect. I cursed the world of spelling and tried erasing it again and saw the paper beginning to wear away. *Balkony.* Suddenly I felt a hand on my shoulder.

"I don't like that word either," Miss Ferenczi whispered, bent over, her mouth near my ear. "It's ugly. My feeling is, if you don't like a word, you don't have to use it." She straightened up, leaving behind a slight odor of Clorets.

At lunchtime we went out to get our trays of sloppy joes, peaches in heavy syrup, coconut cookies, and milk, and brought them back to the classroom, where Miss Ferenczi was sitting at the desk, eating a brown sticky thing she had unwrapped from tightly rubber-banded wax paper. "Miss Ferenczi," I said, raising my hand. "You don't have to eat with us. You can eat with the other teachers. There's a teachers' lounge," I ended up, "next to the principal's office."

"No, thank you," she said. "I prefer it here."

"We've got a room monitor," I said. "Mrs. Eddy." I pointed to where Mrs. Eddy, Joyce and Judy's mother, sat silently at the back of the room, doing her knitting.

"That's fine," Miss Ferenczi said. "But I shall continue to eat here, with you children. I prefer it," she repeated.

"How come?" Wayne Razmer asked without raising his hand.

"I talked with the other teachers before class this morning," Miss Ferenczi said, biting into her brown food. "There was a great rattling of the words for the fewness of ideas. I didn't care for their brand of hilarity. I don't like ditto machine jokes."

"Oh," Wayne said.

"What's that you're eating?" Maxine Sylvester asked, twitching her nose. "Is it food?"

"It most certainly *is* food. It's a stuffed fig. I had to drive almost down to Detroit to get it. I also bought some smoked sturgeon. And this," she said, lifting some green leaves out of her lunchbox, "is raw spinach, cleaned this morning before I came out here to the Garfield-Murry school."

"Why're you eating raw spinach?" Maxine asked.

"It's good for you," Miss Ferenczi said. "More stimulating than soda pop or smelling salts." I bit into my sloppy joe and stared blankly out the window. An almost invisible moon was faintly silvered in the daytime autumn sky. "As far as food is concerned," Miss Ferenczi was saying, "you have to shuffle the pack. Mix it up. Too many people eat . . . well, never mind."

"Miss Ferenczi," Carol Peterson said, "what are we going to do this afternoon?"

"Well," she said, looking down at Mr. Hibler's lesson plan, "I see that your teacher, Mr. Hibler, has you scheduled for a unit on the Egyptians." Carol groaned. "Yessss," Miss Ferenczi continued, "that is what we will do: the Egyptians. A remarkable people. Almost as remarkable as the Americans. But not quite." She lowered her head, did her quick smile, and went back to eating her spinach.

After noon recess we came back into the classroom and saw that Miss Ferenczi had drawn a pyramid on the blackboard, close to her oak tree. Some of us who had been playing baseball were messing around in the back of the room, dropping the bats and the gloves into the playground box, and I think that Ray Schontzeler had just slugged

me when I heard Miss Ferenczi's high-pitched voice quavering with
emotion. "Boys," she said, "come to order right this minute and
take your seats. I do not wish to waste a minute of class time. Take
out your geography books." We trudged to our desks and, still
sweating, pulled out *Distant Lands and Their People.* "Turn to page
forty-two." She waited for thirty seconds, then looked over at Kelly
Munger. "Young man," she said, "why are you still fossicking in your
desk?"

Kelly looked as if his foot had been stepped on. "Why am I
what?"

"Why are you . . . burrowing in your desk like that?"

"I'm lookin' for the book, Miss Ferenczi."

Bobby Kryzanowicz, the faultless brown-noser who sat in the
first row by choice, softly said, "His name is Kelly Munger. He can't
ever find his stuff. He always does that."

"I don't care what his name is, especially after lunch," Miss Ferenczi said. *"Where is your book?"*

"I just found it." Kelly was peering into his desk and with both
hands pulled at the book, shoveling along in front of it several pencils
and crayons, which fell into his lap and then to the floor.

"I hate a mess," Miss Ferenczi said. "I hate a mess in a desk or a
mind. It's . . . unsanitary. You wouldn't want your house at home to
look like your desk at school, now, would you?" She didn't wait for
an answer. "I should think not. A house at home should be as neat as
human hands can make it. What were we talking about? Egypt. Page
forty-two. I note from Mr. Hibler's lesson plan that you have been
discussing the modes of Egyptian irrigation. Interesting, in my view,
but not so interesting as what we are about to cover. The pyramids
and Egyptian slave labor. A plus on one side, a minus on the other."
We had our books open to page forty-two, where there was a picture
of a pyramid, but Miss Ferenczi wasn't looking at the book. Instead,
she was staring at some object just outside the window.

"Pyramids," Miss Ferenczi said, still looking past the window. "I
want you to think about the pyramids. And what was inside. The
bodies of the pharaohs, of course, and their attendant treasures.
Scrolls. Perhaps," Miss Ferenczi said, with something gleeful but un-

smiling in her face, "these scrolls were novels for the pharaohs, helping them to pass the time in their long voyage through the centuries.
But then, I am joking." I was looking at the lines on Miss Ferenczi's
face. "Pyramids," Miss Ferenczi went on, "were the repositories of
special cosmic powers. The nature of a pyramid is to guide cosmic
energy forces into a concentrated point. The Egyptians knew that;
we have generally forgotten it. Did you know," she asked, walking to
the side of the room so that she was standing by the coat closet, "that
George Washington had Egyptian blood, from his grandmother?
Certain features of the Constitution of the United States are notable
for their Egyptian ideas."

Without glancing down at the book, she began to talk about the
movement of souls in Egyptian religion. She said that when people
die, their souls return to Earth in the form of carpenter ants or wal-
nut trees, depending on how they behaved—"well or ill"—in life.
She said that the Egyptians believed that people act the way they do
because of magnetism produced by tidal forces in the solar system,
forces produced by the sun and by its "planetary ally," Jupiter. Jupiter, she said, was a planet, as we had been told, but had "certain properties of stars." She was speaking very fast. She said that the Egyptians were great explorers and conquerors. She said that the greatest
of all the conquerors, Genghis Khan, had had forty horses and forty
young women killed on the site of his grave. We listened. No one
tried to stop her. "I myself have been in Egypt," she said, "and have
witnessed much dust and many brutalities." She said that an old
man in Egypt who worked for a circus had personally shown her an
animal in a cage, a monster, half bird and half lion. She said that this
monster was called a gryphon and that she had heard about them but
never seen them until she traveled to the outskirts of Cairo. She said
that Egyptian astronomers had discovered the planet Saturn, but
had not seen its rings. She said that the Egyptians were the first to
discover that dogs, when they are ill, will not drink from rivers, but
wait for rain, and hold their jaws open to catch it.

"She lies."

We were on the school bus home. I was sitting next to Carl

Whiteside, who had bad breath and a huge collection of marbles. We were arguing. Carl thought she was lying. I said she wasn't, probably.

"I didn't believe that stuff about the bird," Carl said, "and what she told us about the pyramids? I didn't believe that either. She didn't know what she was talking about."

"Oh yeah?" I had liked her. She was strange. I thought I could nail him. "If she was lying," I said, "what'd she say that was a lie?"

"Six times eleven isn't sixty-eight. It isn't ever. It's sixty-six, I know for a fact."

"She said so. She admitted it. What else did she lie about?"

"I don't know," he said. "Stuff."

"What stuff?"

"Well." He swung his legs back and forth. "You ever see an animal that was half lion and half bird?" He crossed his arms. "It sounded real fakey to me."

"It could happen," I said. I had to improvise, to outrage him. "I read in this newspaper my mom bought in the IGA about this scientist, this mad scientist in the Swiss Alps, and he's been putting genes and chromosomes and stuff together in test tubes, and he combined a human being and a hamster." I waited, for effect. "It's called a humster."

"You never." Carl was staring at me, his mouth open, his terrible bad breath making its way toward me. "What newspaper was it?"

"The *National Enquirer*," I said, "that they sell next to the cash registers." When I saw his look of recognition, I knew I had bested him. "And this mad scientist," I said, "his name was, um, Dr. Frankenbush." I realized belatedly that this name was a mistake and waited for Carl to notice its resemblance to the name of the other famous mad master of permutations, but he only sat there.

"A man and a hamster?" He was staring at me, squinting, his mouth opening in distaste. "Jeez. What'd it look like?"

When the bus reached my stop, I took off down our dirt road and ran up through the back yard, kicking the tire swing for good luck. I dropped my books on the back steps so I could hug and kiss our dog,

Mr. Selby. Then I hurried inside. I could smell Brussels sprouts cooking, my unfavorite vegetable. My mother was washing other vegetables in the kitchen sink, and my baby brother was hollering in his yellow playpen on the kitchen floor.

"Hi, Mom," I said, hopping around the playpen to kiss her. "Guess what?"

"I have no idea."

"We had this substitute today, Miss Ferenczi, and I'd never seen her before, and she had all these stories and ideas and stuff."

"Well. That's good." My mother looked out the window behind the sink, her eyes on the pine woods west of our house. Her face and hairstyle always reminded other people of Betty Crocker, whose picture was framed inside a gigantic spoon on the side of the Bisquick box; to me, though, my mother's face just looked white. "Listen, Tommy," she said, "go upstairs and pick your clothes off the bathroom floor, then go outside to the shed and put the shovel and ax away that your father left outside this morning."

"She said that six times eleven was sometimes sixty-eight!" I said. "And she said she once saw a monster that was half lion and half bird." I waited. "In Egypt, she said."

"Did you hear me?" my mother asked, raising her arm to wipe her forehead with the back of her hand. "You have chores to do."

"I know," I said. "I was just telling you about the substitute."

"It's very interesting," my mother said, quickly glancing down at me, "and we can talk about it later when your father gets home. But right now you have some work to do."

"Okay, Mom." I took a cookie out of the jar on the counter and was about to go outside when I had a thought. I ran into the living room, pulled out a dictionary next to the TV stand, and opened it to the G's. *Gryphon:* "variant of griffin." *Griffin:* "a fabulous beast with the head and wings of an eagle and the body of a lion." Fabulous was right. I shouted with triumph and ran outside to put my father's tools back in their place.

Miss Ferenczi was back the next day, slightly altered. She had pulled her hair down and twisted it into pigtails, with red rubber bands holding them tight one inch from the ends. She was wearing a green blouse and pink scarf, making her difficult to look at for a full class day. This time there was no pretense of doing a reading lesson or moving on to arithmetic. As soon as the bell rang, she simply began to talk.

She talked for forty minutes straight. There seemed to be less connection between her ideas, but the ideas themselves were, as the dictionary would say, fabulous. She said she had heard of a huge jewel, in what she called the Antipodes, that was so brilliant that when the light shone into it at a certain angle it would blind whoever was looking at its center. She said that the biggest diamond in the world was cursed and had killed everyone who owned it, and that by a trick of fate it was called the Hope diamond. Diamonds are magic, she said, and this is why women wear them on their fingers, as a sign of the magic of womanhood. Men have strength, Miss Ferenczi said, but no true magic. That is why men fall in love with women but women do not fall in love with men: they just love being loved. George Washington had died because of a mistake he made about a diamond. Washington was not the first *true* President, but she did not say who was. In some places in the world, she said, men and women still live in the trees and eat monkeys for breakfast. Their doctors are magicians. At the bottom of the sea are creatures thin as pancakes which have never been studied by scientists because when you take them up to the air, the fish explode.

There was not a sound in the classroom, except for Miss Ferenczi's voice, and Donna DeShano's coughing. No one even went to the bathroom.

Beethoven, she said, had not been deaf; it was a trick to make himself famous, and it worked. As she talked, Miss Ferenczi's pigtails swung back and forth. There are trees in the world, she said, that eat meat: their leaves are sticky and close up on bugs like hands. She lifted her hands and brought them together, palm to palm. Venus, which most people think is the next closest planet to the sun, is not always closer, and, besides, it is the planet of greatest mystery because of its thick cloud cover. "I know what lies underneath those clouds," Miss Ferenczi said, and waited. After the silence, she said, "Angels.

Angels live under those clouds." She said that angels were not invisible to everyone and were in fact smarter than most people. They did
not dress in robes as was often claimed but instead wore formal evening clothes, as if they were about to attend a concert. Often angels
do attend concerts and sit in the aisles where, she said, most people
pay no attention to them. She said the most terrible angel had the
shape of the Sphinx. "There is no running away from that one,"
she said. She said that unquenchable fires burn just under the surface of the earth in Ohio, and that the baby Mozart fainted dead
away in his cradle when he first heard the sound of a trumpet. She
said that someone named Narzim al Harrardim was the greatest
writer who ever lived. She said that planets control behavior, and
anyone conceived during a solar eclipse would be born with webbed
feet.

"I know you children like to hear these things," she said, "these
secrets, and that is why I am telling you all this." We nodded. It was
better than doing comprehension questions for the readings in
Broad Horizons.

"I will tell you one more story," she said, "and then we will have
to do arithmetic." She leaned over, and her voice grew soft. "There
is no death," she said. "You must never be afraid. Never. That
which is, cannot die. It will change into different earthly and un-
earthly elements, but I know this as sure as I stand here in front of
you, and I swear it: you must not be afraid. I have seen this truth
with these eyes. I know it because in a dream God kissed me.
Here." And she pointed with her right index finger to the side of her
head, below the mouth, where the vertical lines were carved into her
skin.

Absent-mindedly we all did our arithmetic problems. At recess the
class was out on the playground, but no one was playing. We were
all standing in small groups, talking about Miss Ferenczi. We didn't
know if she was crazy, or what. I looked out beyond the playground,
at the rusted cars piled in a small heap behind a clump of sumac, and
I wanted to see shapes there, approaching me.

*　*　*

On the way home, Carl sat next to me again. He didn't say much, and I didn't either. At last he turned to me. "You know what she said about the leaves that close up on bugs?"

"Huh?"

"The leaves," Carl insisted. "The meat-eating plants. I know it's true. I saw it on television. The leaves have this icky glue that the plants have got smeared all over them and the insects can't get off 'cause they're stuck. I saw it." He seemed demoralized. "She's tellin' the truth."

"Yeah."

"You think she's seen all those angels?"

I shrugged.

"I don't think she has," Carl informed me. "I think she made that part up."

"There's a tree," I suddenly said. I was looking out the window at the farms along County Road H. I knew every barn, every broken windmill, every fence, every anhydrous ammonia tank, by heart. "There's a tree that's . . . that I've seen . . ."

"Don't you try to do it," Carl said. "You'll just sound like a jerk."

I kissed my mother. She was standing in front of the stove. "How was your day?" she asked.

"Fine."

"Did you have Miss Ferenczi again?"

"Yeah."

"Well?"

"She was fine. Mom," I asked, "can I go to my room?"

"No," she said, "not until you've gone out to the vegetable garden and picked me a few tomatoes." She glanced at the sky. "I think it's going to rain. Skedaddle and do it now. Then you come back inside and watch your brother for a few minutes while I go upstairs. I need to clean up before dinner." She looked down at me. "You're looking a little pale, Tommy." She touched the back of her hand to my forehead and I felt her diamond ring against my skin. "Do you feel all right?"

"I'm fine," I said, and went out to pick the tomatoes.

Coughing mutedly, Mr. Hibler was back the next day, slipping lozenges into his mouth when his back was turned at forty-five minute intervals and asking us how much of the prepared lesson plan Miss Ferenczi had followed. Edith Atwater took the responsibility for the class of explaining to Mr. Hibler that the substitute hadn't always done exactly what he would have done, but we had worked hard even though she talked a lot. About what? he asked. All kinds of things, Edith said. I sort of forgot. To our relief, Mr. Hibler seemed not at all interested in what Miss Ferenczi had said to fill the day. He probably thought it was woman's talk; unserious and not suited for school. It was enough that he had a pile of arithmetic problems from us to correct.

For the next month, the sumac turned a distracting red in the field, and the sun traveled toward the southern sky, so that its rays reached Mr. Hibler's Halloween display on the bulletin board in the back of the room, fading the scarecrow with a pumpkin head from orange to tan. Every three days I measured how much farther the sun had moved toward the southern horizon by making small marks with my black Crayola on the north wall, ant-sized marks only I knew were there, inching west.

And then in early December, four days after the first permanent snowfall, she appeared again in our classroom. The minute she came in the door, I felt my heart begin to pound. Once again, she was different: this time, her hair hung straight down and seemed hardly to have been combed. She hadn't brought her lunchbox with her, but she was carrying what seemed to be a small box. She greeted all of us and talked about the weather. Donna DeShano had to remind her to take her overcoat off.

When the bell to start the day finally rang, Miss Ferenczi looked out at all of us and said, "Children, I have enjoyed your company in the past, and today I am going to reward you." She held up the small box. "Do you know what this is?" She waited. "Of course you don't. It is a tarot pack."

Edith Atwater raised her hand. "What's a tarot pack, Miss Ferenczi?"

"It is used to tell fortunes," she said. "And that is what I shall do this morning. I shall tell your fortunes, as I have been taught to do."

"What's fortune?" Bobby Kryzanowicz asked.

"The future, young man. I shall tell you what your future will be. I can't do your whole future, of course. I shall have to limit myself to the five-card system, the wands, cups, swords, pentacles, and the higher arcanes. Now who wants to be first?"

There was a long silence. Then Carol Peterson raised her hand.

"All right," Miss Ferenczi said. She divided the pack into five smaller packs and walked back to Carol's desk, in front of mine. "Pick one card from each of these packs," she said. I saw that Carol had a four of cups, a six of swords, but I couldn't see the other cards. Miss Ferenczi studied the cards on Carol's desk for a minute. "Not bad," she said. "I do not see much higher education. Probably an early marriage. Many children. There's something bleak and dreary here, but I can't tell what. Perhaps just the tasks of a housewife life. I think you'll do very well, for the most part." She smiled at Carol, a smile with a certain lack of interest. "Who wants to be next?"

Carl Whiteside raised his hand slowly.

"Yes," Miss Ferenczi said, "let's do a boy." She walked over to where Carl sat. After he picked his five cards, she gazed at them for a long time. "Travel," she said. "Much distant travel. You might go into the Army. Not too much romantic interest here. A late marriage, if at all. Squabbles. But the Sun is in your major arcana, here, yes, that's a very good card." She giggled. "Maybe a good life."

Next I raised my hand, and she told me my future. She did the same with Bobby Kryzanowicz. Kelly Munger, Edith Atwater, and Kim Foor. Then she came to Wayne Razmer. He picked his five cards, and I could see that the Death card was one of them.

"What's your name?" Miss Ferenczi asked.

"Wayne."

"Well, Wayne," she said, you will undergo a *great* metamorphosis, the greatest, before you become an adult. Your earthly element will leap away, into thin air, you sweet boy. This card, this nine of swords here, tells of suffering and desolation. And this ten of wands, well, that's certainly a heavy load."

"What about this one?" Wayne pointed to the Death card.

"That one? That one means you will die soon, my dear." She gathered up the cards. We were all looking at Wayne. "But do not fear," she said. "It's not really death, so much as change." She put the cards on Mr. Hibler's desk. "And now, let's do some arithmetic."

At lunchtime Wayne went to Mr. Faegre, the principal, and told him what Miss Ferenczi had done. During the noon recess, we saw Miss Ferenczi drive out of the parking lot in her green Rambler. I stood under the slide, listening to the other kids coasting down and landing in the little depressive bowl at the bottom. I was kicking stones and tugging at my hair right up to the moment when I saw Wayne come out to the playground. He smiled, the dead fool, and with the fingers of his right hand he was showing everyone how he had told on Miss Ferenczi.

I made my way toward Wayne, pushing myself past two girls from another class. He was watching me with his little pinhead eyes.

"You told," I shouted at him. "She was just kidding."

"She shouldn't have," he shouted back. "We were supposed to be doing arithmetic."

"She just scared you," I said. "You're a chicken. You're a chicken, Wayne. You are. Scared of a little card," I singsonged.

Wayne fell at me, his two fists hammering down on my nose. I gave him a good one in the stomach and then I tried for his head. Aiming my first, I saw that he was crying. I slugged him.

"She was right," I yelled. "She was always right! She told the truth!" Other kids were whooping. "You were just scared, that's all!"

And then large hands pulled at us, and it was my turn to speak to Mr. Faegre.

* * *

In the afternoon Miss Ferenczi was gone, and my nose was stuffed with cotton clotted with blood, and my lip had swelled, and our class had been combined with Mrs. Mantei's sixth-grade class for a crowded afternoon science unit on insect life in ditches and swamps. I knew where Mrs. Mantei lived: she had a new house trailer just down the road from us, at the Clearwater Park. She was no mystery. Somehow she and Mr. Bodine, the other fourth-grade teacher, had managed to fit forty-five desks into the room. Kelly Munger asked if Miss Ferenczi had been arrested, and Mrs. Mantei said no, of course not. All that afternoon, until the buses came to pick us up, we learned about field crickets and two-striped grasshoppers, water bugs, cicadas, mosquitoes, flies, and moths. We learned about insects' hard outer shell, the exoskeleton, and the usual parts of the mouth, including the labrum, mandible, maxilla, and glossa. We learned about compound eyes and the four-stage metamorphosis from egg to larva to pupa to adult. We learned something, but not much, about mating. Mrs. Mantei drew, very skillfully, the internal anatomy of the grasshopper on the blackboard. We learned about the dance of the honeybee, directing other bees in the hive to pollen. We found out about which insects were pests to man, and which were not. On lined white pieces of paper we made lists of insects we might actually see, then a list of insects too small to be clearly visible, such as fleas; Mrs. Mantei said that our assignment would be to memorize these lists for the next day, when Mr. Hibler would certainly return and test us on our knowledge.

CONTRIBUTORS

SHERMAN ALEXIE is a Spokane/Coeur D'Alène Indian. Born in 1966, he has already published eight books of poems, a collection of stories, two novels, and the screenplay for *Smoke Signals,* which had its premiere at the 1998 Sundance Festival. He has been named one of the best young writers in America by *Granta* in 1996 and *The New Yorker* in 1999.

CHARLES BAXTER is the author of a collection of essays, four short story collections, and three novels, the most recent of which, *The Feast of Love,* was published by Pantheon in 2000. "Gryphon" is one of five Baxter stories to appear in *Best American Short Stories.* A native of Minnesota, he lives in Ann Arbor, Michigan.

JUDY BLUME has sold more than seventy million copies of her books and her work has been translated into twenty languages. She is the author of the best-selling novel *Summer Sisters* as well as of such classic books for young readers as *Are You There God? It's Me, Margaret* and *Tales of a Fourth Grade Nothing.* She is an active spokesperson for the National Coalition Against Censorship.

GLO DEANGELIS is a writer as well as educational consultant to Poetry Alive, the national poetry performance troupe. She lives in Asheville, North Carolina, and teaches at a science museum for children.

FRANCESCA DELBANCO received her B.A. from Harvard in 1995 and her M.F.A. from the University of Michigan in 2000. There she won a

Hopwood Award for creative nonfiction. She writes two monthly columns for *Seventeen Magazine* and lives in New York City, where she is at work on a novel.

STUART DYBEK is the author of a book of prose poems and two short story collections: *The Coast of Chicago* and *Childhood and Other Neighborhoods*. In 1996 he received the Pen/Malamud Award for Excellence in the Short Story. "Field Trips" is part of *Saint Stuart,* a collection-in-progress of personal essays about his youth in Chicago.

CAROLYN FERRELL has taught in Germany and New York's Manhattan and the South Bronx and is currently on the faculty of Sarah Lawrence College. She is the author of the short story collection, *Don't Erase Me,* which won the 1997 *Los Angeles Times* book prize for first fiction. Her stories have appeared in numerous journals and magazines, including *Best American Short Stories.*

DAVID HAYNES taught for fifteen years in the public school systems of Minneapolis and Saint Louis. He is a long-time staff member of the National Board for Professional Teaching Standards and the author of two books of juvenile fiction and four novels, including *Somebody Else's Mama* and *All-American Dream Dolls*. In 1996, he was named one of *Granta's* Best of the Young American Novelists.

CAROLINE KETTLEWELL grew up on the campus of an all-boys boarding school in the Blue Ridge Mountains of Virginia. A freelance writer and copywriter, she is the author of *Skin Game: A Cutter's Memoir,* published in 1999 by St. Martin's Press.

MICHAEL PATRICK MACDONALD helped launch Boston's successful gun-buyback program and is founder of the South Boston Vigil Group. He is the author of the memoir *All Souls: A Family Story from Southie*. He lives in South Boston, Massachusetts.

BICH MINH NGUYEN was born in Saigon in 1974 and grew up in Michigan. Her fiction and poetry have appeared in, among other publications, *Scribner's Best of the Fiction Workshops 1999* and *Watermark*.

NINA REVOYR was born in Tokyo in 1969 and grew up in small-town Wisconsin, then later Los Angeles, where she attended public schools. Until recently she has been working for the largest Head Start program in Los Angeles. She is the author of the novel *The Necessary Hunger*.

JEFF RICHARDS was born and raised in Washington, D.C. He has an M.A. in creative writing from Hollins College and currently teaches English at George Washington University. He is associate literary editor of the *Washington Review*.

ABRAHAM RODRIGUEZ JR. dropped out of high school in the South Bronx at sixteen because he was unchallenged and "tired of seeing the heroin addicts hanging out in the hallways." He later earned his high school equivalency and attended City College of New York. He is the author of the novel *Spidertown*.

DAVID SEDARIS, author of *Barrell Fever* and *Naked,* is a diarist, radio commentator, essayist, and short story writer. He has taught writing at the School of Art Institute of Chicago and has held a number of other part-time jobs, including employment as a moving company worker, an apartment cleaner, and an elf in SantaLand at Macy's department store.

PORTER SHREVE grew up in Washington, D.C., and now teaches at the University of Michigan. His novel, *The Obituary Writer,* was published by Houghton Mifflin in 2000. "Neighborhood Watch" is part of a collection-in-progress of linked short stories, *A Brief History of the Fool.*

SUSAN RICHARDS SHREVE is the author of twelve novels, among them *A Country of Strangers, The Train Home,* and most recently, *Plum & Jaggers.* She is also an award-winning children's author and president of the Pen/Faulkner Award for Fiction. In her thirty-five years as an educator, she has taught every level from kindergarten to graduate school.

ASHLEY WARLICK was twenty-two when she won the 1996 Houghton Mifflin Literary Fellowship for her novel *The Distance from the Heart of Things.* Her second novel, *The Summer After June,* was published by Houghton Mifflin in 2000. She lives in North Carolina.

LOIS-ANN YAMANAKA was born in Ho'olehua, Molokai, Hawaii, and lives in Honolulu. She is the author of a verse novella, *Saturday Night at the Pahala Theater,* and three linked novels, all of which are coming-of-age stories told in the pidgin dialect of her native Hawaii. Her most recent book is *Heads by Harry.*

CREDITS